ONE MORE CHALLENGE

The Story Of The Willits Family

Tracy L Willits

iUniverse, Inc.
Bloomington

One More Challenge
The Story Of The Willits Family

iUniverse books may be ordered through booksellers or by contacting:

iUniverse
1663 Liberty Drive
Bloomington, IN 47403
www.iuniverse.com
1-800-Authors (1-800-288-4677)

Because of the dynamic nature of the Internet, any Web addresses or links contained in
this book may have changed since publication and may no longer be valid. The views
expressed in this work are solely those of the author and do not necessarily reflect the
views of the publisher, and the publisher hereby disclaims any responsibility for them.

Any people depicted in stock imagery provided by Thinkstock are models,
and such images are being used for illustrative purposes only.

Certain stock imagery © Thinkstock.

ISBN: 978-1-4620-0413-3 (pbk)
ISBN: 978-1-4620-0412-6 (ebk)

Printed in the United States of America

iUniverse rev. date: 3/28/2011

One More Challenge is the heartwarming
story of a family with 16 children-2 of
them being severely handicapped.

Told from a father's point of view,
the day to day ins and outs, the dramatic
accomplishments and tragedies that
are present in the lives of these
"ordinary people" will surely
catch your interest and
warm your heart

Dedications

There are several people who have had a profound effect on the lives of our family. They have been there to help and offer moral support whenever needed. Although most of these people have passed away I would like to remember them in this dedication.

A very special thanks go out to:

John & Mary friend
Ed & Judy Willits
Father Robert O Steinhausen

Contents

Introduction:
One More Challenge-The Story of The Willits Family

We didn't start out to have sixteen kids, they just kinda came along! We both knew we wanted a large family, (in the 70's & 80's a large family was 6-7 kids!)

I had a good job and my wife was a good mother.

We bought our first house before we were married, (but didn't live together until after the wedding). It all seemed so natural. When our first child came along everything went very easy-easy for me to say anyway-I didn't give birth! My wife Carole handled that quite well. We had a child a year for the next four years after Chris our first son was born. We had five kids in five years!

Then in 1982 we were about to face our first in a long series of challenges that would change our lives forever. Through a process of change that involves faith, hope, and love, we would overcome this, and all of the other challenges that would come before us. Ultimately these changes have made us a stronger family with a very large support network.

We are pleased to share our story with you.

The Willits family

CHAPTER 1:
IN THE BEGINNING

Who I was

I was kind of a reckless guy at least by today's standards. I had dropped out of college to pursue a career in the retail grocery industry with an international company.

I had grown up in the auto industry. My father was a used car salesman, an honest one which meant that he didn't sell refrigerators to Eskimos but had a good repeat clientele. I used to spend some of my after school hours and a lot of the summer hours at the car lot- I would talk to my dad for a bit, but when the other salesman came in I had to leave (I wasn't forced to leave, I just couldn't stand all the BS!) I ended up hanging around the shop where the mechanics repaired the cars-no OSHA or liability issues in those days! It was great!! They wouldn't let me work on the cars as it was also a new car dealership but I learned quite a bit about mechanics and the fundamentals of how the cars and trucks worked-or didn't work! This knowledge would come to be very helpful throughout my life (at least so far!)

Race Car Driver!!!

I was always a pretty hard working guy. I had a paper route when I turned the magic age (ten in those days,) I kept my route and added a couple as time went on. I didn't give up my routes until I got my first real job. It was part time at a local restaurant. I stayed there for a year until I went to work for an international food retailer. I would stay in this industry for over twenty years.

While I was working for Safeway (earning great money) I realized one of my dreams. I bought and built a racecar!! It was a 1961 Plymouth Fury. It had a 318 engine with an automatic transmission-those Chrysler transmissions were bullet proof, at least back then. I removed all of the glass and put in a T-Handle Harness which was all that was required back in those days. I was starting out in the amateur class where I would remain just until I did well enough to get a better car and a sponsor to be able to move up. I raced at Playland Park in Council Bluffs Iowa (today it is a city recreation park.)

The 1974 racing season started out kind of lackluster-for me anyway. Before your first race they let you go out and drive around the track a couple of times to get used to the conditions and the atmosphere-large crowd included!

My first couple of races I spent getting used to the conditions. The track was a quarter mile track (if that!) You could only get up to about sixty or seventy miles an hour on the straight-aways and you really had to watch the turns. When your going down the straightaway at sixty-five miles an hour and someone hits you from the rear (called rubbing!) it is a strange feeling. It took me a couple of races just to get used to that! After a couple of outings (you would race two-four times an outing depending on how well you did), I started to move up and start placing-they used to start paying at about fifth or sixth place. I forget, but all I knew was that I started getting money!!

About halfway through the first season I was in the pole position and in the lead for the very first time! We had two laps to go and————some idiot spun out and came back onto the track going the wrong way! He hit me head on (unfortunately it was in the straightaway) and since I was leading the pack (first time ever!) The cars behind me also hit me. I was dazed after it all. I couldn't get my car to start (I would find out later why!) My pit crew had to help push the car off of the track and onto the trailer to take it home.

My pit crew consisted of some good friends and I paid them with the customary twelve pack of beer (which we all had to split). Upon a closer inspection of the car I discovered that the front end collision had pushed the bumper and grille back about a foot. That however, was nothing compared to the rear end collision in which area I lost about a foot and a half. I was now driving a compact-I wonder if they'll let me drop down to that class?When I finally got the hood open I found the engine just lying loose inside the compartment. That was it! I didn't really have the facilities to repair the car. I had financed everything myself as it was-racing can be pretty expensive-even in those days!!

Racing comes to an end!!

That's ok! I still loved to hunt, fish, and hike-anything outside. I had a gun collection (sold to finance purchase of first house), and a canoe with tons of fishing equipment.

Getting Serious!

I was still working at Safeway when one of my co-workers brought one of her friends to the store with her. She was cute. She had long brown hair and a pretty good figure. She was still in high school. I was 21 at the time and was fairly worldly-at least socially anyway-you get my drift. At the time I was actually dating the co-worker's older sister. That relationship didn't really go anywhere and I had another not long after with the same result.

FUDPUCKERS!! I was at a party not long after and someone asked if I had ever had a FudPucker? I said no, having no idea of what they meant-was this a pet, a food, or a beverage-beverage-yeah right! We're at a party!! They (I don't remember who) mixed up a batch of these. They tasted great and went down very easily-can't be very potent. Guess again! After about three of these (still can't remember) I was on the floor, someone said I had my arms around the legs of a pretty girl-probably around her feet at that point!

That was the first time I missed work. I didn't wake up until 11:00am the next morning-what's in those?I always used to tease the guys and girls (equal opportunity) when they would come in sick with a hangover. Now it was my turn to call the kettle black. I still have the recipe for these!

After that experience I thought it best to slow down a bit. I wanted a good relationship that would last-at least for a little while. My co-worker brought her friend to the store again and I started talking to her. Before long we were out on a date. The rest is history.

One of the things that I liked about Carole is that she is a "real Person." She does not try to put on a "show" or be anything other than who she is. When you get married I don't care if it's the first time or the hundredth time, you change in some ways. That's part of the adjusting process that is so ever-important to a happy and lasting relationship. You grow together as a couple, still remembering who you are as an individual. Carole was and still is a very sweet person-almost too sweet sometimes. We hit it off well and after spilling water on the pizza (first date-I won't say who.) We always had fun together and enjoyed each other's company. She liked being outdoors as well but was not very athletic (I guess I was athletic enough for both of us).We would go on the usual dates but also do outdoor stuff as well.

In May of 1975, we had a terrible tornado in Omaha. I was living in an apartment building and was worried that Carole may be alone at home. I went over to her house to make sure everything was ok. Her dad thought I was nuts-as I look back on this I will plead temporary insanity! I was in love though and the worst thing I could imagine would be to lose her. We got engaged shortly after that.

3

Getting Married

We got engaged right after Carole graduated from high school. We set an October wedding date, but her parents thought we should wait-at least till spring. We stuck to our guns (or bells in this case) and were married in October of 1975, at Our Lady of Lourdes Catholic Church in Omaha. It was a beautiful church wedding. We are still members of that parish and it looks much the same now as when we were married thirty five years ago. We put in new pews a couple of years back and the church sold the old ones. Guess who bought one? It is in our upstairs sunroom. We also bought the church organ. It was the original pump organ that was up in the choir loft.

We had the rehearsal dinner at my parent's house. It was very casual and comfortable. Carole had a large family (six brothers and sisters-combined!) and quite a few cousins, aunts, and uncles. On my side it was my parents and my brother and his wife and my friends and co-workers.

After the wedding we were driven to the reception in my father's Gold Cadillac-way coooolll!! The reception was a large affair as well. Between Carole's family and my friends and co-workers it was a sight to be seen!

Our First House

We had decided that summer that we wanted a house to live in. We were on a pretty tight budget and looked at several, but couldn't afford them. We ran into a fixer-upper not far from the church and neighborhood that Carole had grown up in. It was affordable, and after liquidating some personal items we were able to buy the house. There was also a small bungalow out back that was rented out. The little house was in pretty good shape and had been kept up. We were able to rent that out and make half of the house payment from that alone!

You talk about a fixer-upper!! The main house was built in 1880 and had been rental property (owned by a US Senator) and as such had been greatly neglected for years. It still had the old octopus furnace (gravity-coal fed) in the center of the dirt-floor basement. The rest of the neighborhood was great! The houses were all kept up well-a typical older neighborhood in south Omaha.

The tenants who were living in the house didn't want to leave. They had been there forever and been paying a token amount of rent and had been "keeping up" the property. They were definitely a group-looked like something right out of "Lil Abner"! You had Ma & Pa Kettle and the boys. We believe that they had been sneaking back into the place for a couple of weeks after we moved in but could never catch them or prove anything. One day while I was at work Carole was in the basement cleaning up when she heard the back door open and close and footsteps across the kitchen floor (upstairs) . She thought that I had gotten off work early. She called my name from the basement and was surprised and a little frightened when the person walked back out the back door rather quickly. Then the door slammed shut! I came home about an hour later and she told me about "her afternoon!" We changed the locks and that ended it!

Rebuilding The House

Our first fixer-upper was going to be a real doozie! Where do you start when everything has been so run down. The basement had a dirt floor and as a result the entire house was very dirty and dusty. The previous tenants had left all of their unwanted (and totally unusable items in and around the house. There were no walkthroughs in those days. After we finished cleaning it up (took two weeks and five truckloads to the dump) we decided that we should have heat to start with. You should always have the necessities first. Obviously our first project was to replace the octopus furnace and install central air. We got a home improvement loan and installed a new furnace, ductwork, and central air conditioning. We had to have that done by professionals as that was way past my scope at least at that point. However, before that could be accomplished we had to have a concrete floor to set it on. When we moved in the basement floor was dirt. Have you ever tried to sweep a dirt floor? It doesn't work very well!

I was very lucky in that Carole's father, brothers, and brothers-in-law were very handy and several actually worked in the construction trade. We graded and poured a new basement floor, and, for the next three years we would spend a lot of time bringing the rest of the house back to cognitive life. We built a new garage, rewired the house, and put new plumbing in the house. I would learn all of the skills necessary to be self-sustaining as far as doing all of the repairs and remodeling on a house. In addition to the above I learned how to do concrete work including paving, basement floors, and foundation repair and setting. I also learned carpentry-measure once and cut twice or something like that!

Then we painted the outside and then started on the interior walls. There was wallpaper on all of the walls, (they never painted inside walls 100+ years ago). When we tried to remove it we found that some of the walls were coming off with the paper. Plan B! We instead covered the downstairs (except for the kitchen) with one-quarter-inch drywall. I learned to apply, joint, and finish drywall before we were done-looked great!! The upstairs was a different story. We removed the wall paper and just patched and painted the walls and ceilings.

I bought a truck to help haul the building materials around and to make trips to the landfill with our "construction surplus items." I bought a "real truck." The 1953 Chevy pickup was not only a "real truck' but a real old truck as well. It did run great and never failed us. I would have to sell this "gem" when Chris was born as we couldn't put a child seat in the front seat-no seat belts! I would miss this truck! It had the six cylinder engine and the four speed transmission with granny-low. Other than the child seat thing the only other drawback was that it didn't handle very well at interstate speeds. There are trade-offs in life. We sometimes have to give up things that we have come to like in order to better support the things (or people in this case) that we love. Being a family person means that you love your family above even your most cherished possessions.

Riding Lawnmower!

We've all wanted one of these! Now that I had my own house I went ahead and bought one. It was a Sears craftsman eight-horsepower riding mower with a floating deck. There was just one problem; while our yard was bigger than a postage stamp, it definitely was not big enough or laid out for a riding lawnmower. It didn't take long for me to realize my mistake (Carole and everyone else had seen it from the beginning!) The final straw was when I got stuck going up the two foot high bank in the front yard-spun my wheels (in more ways than one!) and tore up the yard even more! Don't get me wrong, it did a great job (in about thirty seconds!)

I ended up trading it for the building materials for the garage. I actually made out pretty good on this! We would have much bigger yards in the years to come and I have never wanted another riding lawn mower-just got it out of my system I guess!

I had always thought that it would be the "Cat's Meow" to have a nice house with a well kept and manicured yard. I didn't realize how much work is involved just to keep a yard looking good. Throw small kids into that equation and it's next to impossible-unless you're retired or have an almost part-time job! We not only had a lawn to keep up, but trees (older larger ones) and shrubs. It seemed like I was a glutton for punishment! We kept everything up but it was far from manicured! Still to this day we keep the grass, trees, and bushes trimmed but we are not YARDAHOLICS (is that a word?) It has gotten better since most of the kids are older and out on their own.

Chris, Our First Child Is On The Way!

Carole had a doctor's visit and our first child was on the way. I was the younger of two boys and had never been around a baby before. I had no idea what to expect or how to handle the situation. Carole on the other hand had always been around babies and small children. She came from a family of seven children and had many cousins of all ages.

As our pregnancy progressed (I found that out quick!) I learned all of the do's and don'ts that go along with having a pregnant wife. You do still take walks together. You don't have her help you move furniture! You do still have marital bliss. You don't have marital bliss after the fifth month! You do go out and get whatever she is craving. You don't get angry with her for getting her cravings. And so on so forth.

I was surprised to see how much her stomach grew. By the time Chris was born she looked like she was going to pop! Something else I had never seen or even heard about were stretch marks. It looked like Carole's outer layer of skin was trying to separate! This was truly a great learning experience for me.

Just in Time!

Our first child was born in the next year. Chris was a very happy and healthy baby-still is as an adult!I had just finished the nursery the day before Carole went into labor. I still had to put on the door-that would wait for a couple of weeks. I was out hunting for night crawlers (fish bait). It had rained the day before and that always brings them to the top. When Carole went into labor-I asked her if she could wait until I had found more night crawlers but she insisted that we go right away. She was never a serious fisherman! I told her Okay, I would wait to go fishing!!

Carole had a suitcase already packed and we made it to the hospital way before the doctor. They didn't let you go into the delivery room then (even with fishing poles!) When the doctor brought Chris out for me to see I remember saying that he had an egg-shaped head. The doctor assured me that that was something that sometimes happens at birth. He told me that he would look normal tomorrow-he was right-I let him keep his medical degree!! He shook my hand and congratulated me. A newborn baby is so small! Tiny arms and legs and even tinier fingers and toes!

I still remember the first time I held Chris in my arms. You are holding a new life that you helped to create for the very time. I took a day off of work and when I went back everyone could tell I was a very proud first-time father (the cigars I handed out may have helped to give it away!) By the time we were through having babies I could have owned a cigar store-it would have been way cheaper!

Back then, after giving birth you stayed in the hospital for three or four nights. We brought Chris home (I let Carole come too) and our first home was complete. He was a very happy baby and slept through the night from day one! He did have a spell a couple of weeks later where he would cry in the middle of the night-that's when the nursery door went back on-at four AM in the morning!!

It was then that we learned the first cardinal rule that all parents have learned for thousands of years. When you have a baby you can't just pick up and go somewhere like before. It doesn't matter if you are driving a car, riding in a covered wagon, or trekking across the desert as in biblical times. The same rule still holds true. You have to pack a diaper bag. What is that all about!? I didn't remember my mom and dad packing one for me! In the diaper bag are all of the essentials for a baby. You brought diapers (we used cloth at that time.) A plastic bag for the dirty diapers was also necessary. You also needed a washcloth (not for your face!) An extra change of clothes was also a good idea if you were going to be more than an hour or two. Extra bottles were also in order. Next thing we learned was when you have two children or babies still in diapers you just needed a bigger diaper bag!

Carole didn't work at that time so if Chris woke up during the night we had a deal. If he (or any of the others as time went on) would wake up after four AM I would see to their needs, I had to be to work at seven AM so I had to be up pretty soon anyway. If they woke up before four AM Carole would see to their needs. This would be our plan for all of the kids.

I remember one night (or early morning) Chris had been up all night and I decided to give Carole a break and try to comfort Chris. I was talking to him softly when all of the sudden he opened up like a geyser! Unfortunately I was holding him close when I was talking to him. He looked like a fountain! The once swallowed formula came right back up with tremendous velocity. It didn't taste very good the second time around-at least in my opinion. I didn't have time to close my mouth! Carole was awake by that time and standing at the nursery door. She tried not to laugh but just couldn't hold it in. I didn't understand that-I wasn't laughing!

Other than that one incident (I did forgive him) Chris was a joy to have from the start and has not changed in thirty-four years. We were constant companions in my off-work times. I had a child seat in the front seat of my pickup truck for him. We also kept a baggie of chocolate chip cookies in the cab of the truck for him (not the old Chevy). When I was working on the house (most of my time off!), he had one of those little wooden workbenches with the play hammer and pegs and he would "help" me although at the time I'm not sure that I knew much more than he did! We also dressed alike. I would wear those overalls like the train engineers wore-the kind with the suspenders. We bought the same outfit for Chris. When I would work on the house I would wear mine and when he was "helping" me he would wear his too.

I had been taking the classes to convert to Catholicism. Chris and I were baptized together at the Easter Vigil in 1976. It was later that year sometime between Thanksgiving and Christmas when Carole told me she might be pregnant again. Eric was on the way! I worked full time at work and almost full time at home trying to get the "Green Room" done. The green room would be Chris' bedroom so Eric could have the nursery. The nursery was obviously just that. It was a smaller bedroom on the second floor with a sloping ceiling.

This would be our first Christmas with a child. We knew we would have more kids (DUH!!). We decided right away that we needed ground rules for Christmas so as not to get carried away (pretty easy to do this time of year!) We would buy 1 large gift, 1 medium size gift, and 1 small gift (stocking stuffer) for each child. At first we set the spending limit at $50 for each child (we would adhere to that limit for the next 5-6 years.)

Christmas Parties at Grandma's

We would start a tradition this year (1976) that would continue on for over thirty years. On Christmas Eve our family and my brother Bob's family (my parents had two boys-me and Bob-no sisters) would meet at our parents' house for Christmas. We would exchange gifts (at first-our family was still small enough not to bankrupt everyone!) and catch up on the events since the last time we saw each other. My parents would go all-out at Christmas. There would be quite a spread-oysters, pickled herring, wine, and more special treats than I can remember! It was truly an event that we would remember forever-or at least until the next years gathering. Even after my father passed away my mother would continue to have the Christmas Eve parties at the family house for the next eleven years.

My brother Bob and his wife Elaine also had their first child born that year As well. Their daughter, Kara, was a week older than our first son Chris.

New Arrival

The stork would be working overtime for the next twenty years at the Willits house! Chris started walking about the time Eric was born. Chris was a big brother! He handled the job very well and set an excellent example. Chris and Eric got along great and still do as do all of our kids.

Eric came fast. From the time Carole went into labor until the time Eric was in my arms (I got to go in for this one) was less than three hours. I didn't even have time to think about going night crawler hunting this time!Eric was also a very happy baby. We took him home and it was basically the same story as Chris. He slept through the night from day 1! Most of our kids would share this GREAT habit. Eric had a totally different look than Chris. He had blond hair and blue eyes, where as Chris was darker complexioned (just like me,) and had brown hair and brown eyes.

The House is Coming Along Great!

By this time the old "Rebuilder" was looking pretty good. We had just finished painting the outside, the inside was done (at least to our liking), and the lawn was looking great. We had planted shrubs around the front porch and I had repaired the damage from the riding lawnmower. It fit right in with the rest of the neighborhood. It was probably fifty years since that had last occurred!

It had very good "Curb appeal" as well. Along with the fresh paint and landscaping we put in a new sidewalk and driveway to match the garage. It had a certain charm that I really wouldn't describe as antique but more old fashioned and very functional. At one time this was the farmhouse for the surrounding land back in the 1880's. The actual neighborhood wasn't really developed until about 1900 or so. There were two vent type openings in the attic facing north and south. Carole had asked me once about them and why they weren't glass windows. I explained to her that they were meant as a defense from any hostile Indians that may attack the farmstead. She believed me!! At least for a while!

New House

The year went by very fast, rebuilding a one-hundred year old house and having two small kids! I got an extra present at Christmas time. Carole told me she was pregnant-again. Todd was on the way! We got the house totally redone that winter and early spring (1977-78).We needed to take a second look at our situation. Our house was actually in very good shape now, but it was shrinking-just like that 80's show with Lily Tomlin! I had gotten a couple of promotions at work and my income had grown to the point where we were in a larger tax bracket as well. We decided to look for a larger, newer house.I had spent all my spare time working on our first fixer-upper house that I didn't have much time to relax or do other things with the kids, in fact I had only been fishing once or twice in the last three years!

Our first house-the rebuilder!

We looked at several new and NEWER homes (when your house is one-hundred years old it's hard to find an OLDER home). We just wanted a newer house that we wouldn't have to work on all the time (not necessarily true). We found one we just loved. It was in a suburb of Omaha. It was on a quiet cul de sac and there were lots of other kids on the block. It was not a brand new house but was definitely newer than what we were used to. It was twenty years old. Out back was a large open area that had been planned for a subdivision. However, it was lower and most of it was on a flood plain so the building plans were scrapped. It was like living on acreage without all of the work!

As time went on I would take the kids hiking through the field. It was pretty large, about a quarter mile wide and a half mile long. There was a creek running right through the middle of it. When the boys were old enough I would take them down to the creek with BB guns and teach them to target shoot. It was great! The creek was tree lined and afforded some shade on otherwise hot summer days. It was not very deep. A small child could actually stand in the middle and only get their feet wet. The field on either side was all grass.

We moved in on July 1, 1978. I wouldn't have to do any major work probably for the next twenty to thirty years (or so I thought!) The new house was already in great shape. The paint on the outside while not new was very good. On the south side was a tiered garden with plants and flowers. The back yard was larger than the one we had in Omaha. There was also a covered patio out . The basement was a walkout in the rear to the covered patio.

It was a typical split entry home with an upstairs or main floor and a basement. Inside there were four bedrooms, two up and two down. When Todd was born he could have his own room! That however, wouldn't last very long! There was also a very large family room above the garage. It had beamed ceilings and dark wood walls (Paneling-very good quality). The kitchen and dining room were also on the upper floor.

The lower floor had the other two bedrooms along with a rec room. It was just as big as the family room upstairs and had the walkout door to the covered patio. We would eventually cut this in half and make another bedroom downstairs.

Todd was born in August of 1978. Todd resembled Eric with his blond hair and blue eyes. I was starting to watch the blond haired neighbors a little closer-especially the men! Todd was a little different from Chris and Eric. He was always trying to "push the envelope" wondering what mountain he could climb next? This year really went fast too!! Around Christmas time Carole once again gave me that little smile! Katrina was on the way. We had plenty of room. We were ready!

Our second house

Also in 1978 we took some of the money we made on our first house and bought a new car and truck. We had always bought used before and wanted to try new ones. What a mistake! We were very disappointed in both. We will never do that again! At this point we were still living well below our means —How I miss those days!

It was after New Years that Carole once again had a doctor's visit. She didn't drive at this point so I had to drive her to the appointments. There was a long wait for these appointments. The doctor would schedule three people each hour no matter how long each would take. There were times that we would wait for over two hours just to be seen by the doctor. If he had a delivery he would have to leave and come back. You can just imagine the frustration we (mostly me-I was giving up my only day off!) felt.When Carole came out of the doctors office I didn't even have to ask anymore. She would give me that special smile. By now I was well aware of just what that meant! Katrina was on the way!

Katrina was born near the end of our fourth year of marriage. She came out smiling and has never stopped! I remember holding her for the first time in the delivery room. I was holding a little girl -our first little girl. The inner joy that I felt from that very memorable event was immeasurable.

We soon discovered that the hand-me-downs from boys couldn't satisfy the dress requirements for a little girl! We were also at the point where with four kids it was almost impossible to find a babysitter other than other family members. It put a cramp on our social life-although that has always been secondary with us. When Katrina was ten years old she was probably more skilled at taking care of babies and small children than most women twenty years her senior! She was also an animal lover-especially dogs! She would scout the want ads for four-legged homeless critters. If she found one that sounded like it would work she would alert Carole (also a dog lover!) They would go on their "secret mission" to rescue the dog (or cat) from obscurity.

The River Cabin

We still had some extra money left over from the sale of the first house. We used this to buy a cabin. It was a large house trailer with a sleeping porch built on. It was just off the Missouri River about forty-five minutes north of Omaha. It was great! We could come here on the weekends and even some nights as it was so close. It was the ideal setup. There was a channel parallel to the river about one hundred fifty yards in with a connecting channel to the river. Our cabin sat on a high bank so there was no danger of flooding. We actually would go duck hunting in the channel in the late fall and early winter and fish in the spring and summer. We bought a boat, a river Jon boat. It had an engine and could actually go on the MissouriRiver. I was never at ease traveling on the river in this boat as it was just seemed to be too open. One day while I was traveling down the river the boat (and I) hit a whirlpool. It just moved the boat (and me) over about five feet. It was a very strange feeling! Another time I was taking the kids out for a boat ride in the channel- we wouldn't take them on the river until they were older. We ran out of gas and moved to the bank. I threw the anchor over to the bank to help hold the boat. Guess what!!? I forgot to tie the other end of the anchor rope to the boat. The anchor went ashore alright along with all of the rope. I got wet that day. That's all I'm going to say! Everyone else thought that it was very funny and couldn't stop laughing. I was still wondering what they were laughing about? I still get teased about this from time to time-even after thirty years!!

Discipline

When you have children, I don't care how many-1 or 50, you need to set boundaries. We used corporal punishment-spanking. We wouldn't use belts or sticks or anything like that, just our open hands. We started to use discipline at an early age. By the time the kids were four or five years old they would be spanked if they had done something that we had told them not to. It may seem a bit early to start disciplinary action but we found that we seldom had to discipline them at all when they were older-ten or above. They would do as we asked them for most part the first or second time. When the kids got older (ten and above) we would ground them and/or have them do extra chores around the house-at that point the spankings would have hurt us more than them!

The other thing that is imperative is that when a married couple disciplines children they must have a united front. Carole and I would go into our bedroom and discuss what we thought was the appropriate discipline for the transgression that had been committed. We would have the kids wait in the living or dining room while we decided what to do. That served two purposes. It would give them a chance to think about what they did and they would sometimes become a little nervous. It also gave us a chance to take a "breath" to make sure that we weren't jumping the gun and being too hasty or harsh. Parents can sometimes "over discipline" their children. We were always consistent with discipline. "The same time for the same crime!" or something like that-you can tell that Carole's father was a policeman!

The Willits Railroad (Model Railroad)

One of the other hobbies that I had was a model railroad. My father had bought me a Lionel train set and table as a child. I loved it so it was no surprise when I wanted a setup "For the kids." I talked my wife into this under the guise of "the kids will love it!" They did, but not as much as I did-Carole had me figured out from the start! It started out as a four foot oval in our living room and ended up as a 19' x 5' layout in the basement. The older kids helped me a lot with this as we added on and progressed with the construction (mini construction). We had all of the little buildings that would light up along with the little people with cars and trucks.

The actual track and train set up was pretty neat as well. We didn't put too much emphasis on the trains or track. It was a pretty scale looking layout. We put two tracks side by side all the way around the outside. The kids loved this as they would race trains. They couldn't understand why the inside train always won!

We would bring this layout to the house on 30th Avenue and set it up in the basement. Since then we have moved to a smaller house. It is now in boxes awaiting the proper time and place for a revival reconstruction! It would make a great family project for not only the kids, but, also the grandchildren as well.

Cowboy Boots

We bought the boys cowboy boots when they were about 2-3 years old. I didn't realize they made them that small! We would end up buying them for all of the kids including the girls for years to come! These were more expensive than the regular shoes but could be worn in the winter and snow and turned out to be very practical and well worth the extra expense.

The kids loved them. It's hilarious to watch a small child walk down the street in the summer with shorts, no shirt, and cowboy boots!My granddaughters still do this to this day (with a shirt!) We just recently purchased a pair for Veronica and a pair for Kaylee. They love them! Truly a family legacy!

The Willits Children-Christmas 1980-notice the cowboy boots!!

A Basketball Team!

This year just as the other three went by pretty fast. There was no "surprise" (announcement) at Christmas time this year. Whew!! We needed a break. The surprise announcement instead came at Easter.

Chad was on the way! The year was 1980. The kids were starting to make friends and play with the other neighbor kids by now. We lived on a very quiet cul de sac.

Chad was born in the fall of 1980. He was our largest child weighing in a little over 8 LBS. Just like the others he was a fairly easy delivery. Chad was and still is a very conscientious person. He always put himself last, and would always follow through with his obligations-and still does to this day. He earned the nickname "monkey" for his ability to climb the tallest cabinets (in the kitchen) to rescue snacks and treats from obscurity! We would find no hiding place existed that Chad could not conquer. Chad always seemed to have a smile on his face as did most of our children.

Fireman of The Year!

In the spring of 1980 we were sitting on the porch one evening watching the kids play in the neighbors' yard. Chris, Eric, and Todd were wrestling around when Todd seemed to just go limp. By the time we got over there he was kind of pale and clammy. We called the rescue squad and by the time they arrived Todd was coming around. One of the fireman said that he had just gotten the wind knocked out of him. We took him to the hospital to get checked out and found that was indeed the case.

I felt totally helpless in this situation. I had always wanted to be able to "fix" everything. When it came time to "fix" (or at least help) Todd I couldn't do it. I ended up joining the local Volunteer Fire Department in 1980. I thought that having a fairly large family (at this point anyway) I needed to have some medical training. They provide that for free. Our neighbor across the street was heavily involved in the department and we were friends (no blond hair) as well so he took me under his wing.

For the first year I went through the mandatory initial training which consisted of First Aid classes, the very basics of fire fighting, operating the fire and rescue vehicles, and so on. We went to Fire School the next year. It was held in Grand Island Nebraska in the summer. I took High Speed Emergency Driving, and Fire Fighter I. At night we joined together with other volunteer fireman from across the state to exchange stories and experiences. We learned a great deal and it was a lot of fun.

In general I really enjoyed being on the department, but there were a few disappointments as well. I had never seen a deceased person close up except at funerals. Also, being an all volunteer department there were some politics involved. I was never a good politician. I just figured that if you did your job to the best of your ability there would be no need to cover your behind.

I became an EMT and drove the rescue squad. I still remember the first time we went into a real burning house (or apartment as this was), the heat was unbearable-like nothing you could ever imagine! We had our gear which consisted of a heavy coat, long fire pants with suspenders, long boots, a helmet, heavy gloves, and an air pack. I made a lot of calls and made a sizeable contribution to the department in man hours as well. It really felt good that I was making a difference in our community.

I was selected as "Fireman of the Year" for 1981. The next year I was decorated for my part in aiding in the resolution of a hostage incident involving a family with small children. It was the kind of thing that happens to "everyone else" in "someone else's" neighborhood.

Hostage Situation

A father was visiting his children on a Saturday night-he was divorced and it was just a casual visitation. His ex-wife had a new boyfriend who happened to drive by her house and see the ex-husband's truck in the driveway. It didn't help that the boyfriend was high on drugs at the time! The boyfriend went to his apartment and loaded two 12 gauge pump shotguns and proceeded to go back to the girlfriend's (or ex-wife depending on where you stood) house. With one of the shotguns he blew off the side door-no need to use the knob! He proceeded downstairs where the father was watching television with his two small children. He shot the father twice at close range with the other shotgun. One shot hit the father in the side of the shoulder, and the other was aimed at his heart. He was able to deflect most of that shot by raising his arm just at the right time. He was very seriously wounded and didn't have much time. Miraculously the kids, who were sitting one on each side of their father, were not hit. They were very bloody but it was all of their father's blood. By this time the police were on the scene as well as we were. The man refused to come out of the house or to let anyone else out. He finally let us come in (he had the second shotgun pointed at us the whole time) and take the father to the hospital. As soon as we got him out of the house we talked to the police and gave them the layout of the house and the logistics of the situation. I had never seen such a severe shooting victim that was still alive. We got him into the squad. I drove the squad while my neighbor (who was a paramedic) tended to his wounds. We were all very surprised to hear that not only did he survive, but that he made a full recovery.

It was a very meaningful time in my life. I had learned that I could make a difference outside of work and my family. Unfortunately all of that would soon change-something I had no control over.

Chapter II:
Our First Challenge

Our First Challenge-No Job!

In the late summer of 1981 Carole gave me that smile again. I knew it by heart at this point. Becky was on the way. Her due date would be the second week of May in 1982.

I was cashing a retirement check for one of our customers at one of the stores; it was a Monday Morning in January of 1982. The lady counts her money (she was retired from a bank!), puts it in her billfold, looks up at me and says "we're sure going to miss you guys". Thinking that she was older and may be moving down south to a milder climate, I asked her "where are you going?" She looked up at me with a puzzled look and said "honey, you haven't heard?! They're closing the stores!" I asked her where she had heard that and she said it was on the radio. We turned on the radio in the office and at 11:20 that morning and heard the confirmation message. We immediately called the district manager. He wasn't taking any calls-big lump in the stomach!! He made it around to all of his stores by the end of the day to tell everyone personally-not something to be done over the phone (or radio!). I'll remember the events of this day for the rest of my life!

I thought to myself "this can't be happening." What are we going to do? How can I tell my wife? As it turns out I didn't have to tell her. My brother in law also worked for the same company and her sister had already heard and reported the news to Carole. I went home that day very depressed (who wouldn't be!!?)

We had five weeks. The last working day would be March 2, 1982. As it turned out a lot of the people were let go early as business dropped quite a bit just in the first week. I got to stay till the end. You talk about a somber atmosphere!!! It's times like this that you realize that the people that you are working with are real flesh and blood beings. The disappointments, the

19

hopes, the possibilities all come into play here. Some of us (including me) were offered a chance to transfer to other areas of the country with the company. I refused. What stuck in my mind and always will was that little old lady telling me about the massive closure, and I, not having a clue as to what she was talking about. I figured if they did that here, they would do it in other places too-and they did. Not a very good business practice-especially from a company that was supposed to be the world-wide leader in food retailing!

Some of the people took the transfers. They received very little help relocating-no moving expenses and such. Most of them came back here broke, (mentally as well as financially!) In looking back I believe that this closure played a big part in a lot of family breakups. These jobs, even the lesser paying ones were pretty lucrative. The job market at the time was very depressed. A lot of the people had to take jobs paying half of what they were used to or even minimum wage ($3.35 @ hr at that time).

I was pretty lucky. I got severance pay and my vacation pay which equaled about 3 months of paychecks. I was really lucky (or took a big chance-gambler). I took a job as a part time route man with a national bread company. My pay rate was nothing to brag about but I did a good job and had the next available route-two weeks later. I really liked route work and picked it up right away. I had to get up early (always did anyway) but I would also get done earlier in the day as well (at least most days.) I worked into management within the first six months and we really never skipped a beat. I was full time with insurance by the time Becky was born-only two months later. The only thing that I regret about this was that I had to quit the Volunteer Fire Department. I really enjoyed the service and camaraderie.

Becky was born pretty much on schedule and was a fairly quick delivery. As she would grow older and start to develop she would become a very pretty young girl-still is. She had a more athletic build than Katrina (not fat or anything-just really in shape!)

Our Parents-The Kids Grandparents

We were both pretty lucky in that our parents were very supportive and good, honest people. It made everything a lot easier. Carole's parents and in-laws would give us the necessary help in rebuilding the house. My parents were always there to provide moral and social support. It may not seem important but it is. Both sets of parents would continue to do this.

Both of our fathers had been alcoholics for years. Both had quit drinking in their later years-the main reason our family (my mom and dad, my brother, and I) had struggled for so many years. Carole's father went through treatment and actually became an alcoholism counselor! My father took a different path. One day he was taking a shower and fainted in the bathtub (he hadn't been drinking yet that day.) He struck his head on the side of the tub and my mother called the rescue squad. He found out that he was a diabetic. The doctor told him that if he did not stop drinking he would be dead within a year. The year was 1976. Both my brother Bob and I had our first children on the way-but not yet here. My father was determined to see his grandchildren born. He quit drinking-cold turkey! No AA, no treatment, no medication. That truly took a lot of will power! We would find out much later why he had become an alcoholic in the first place-at least our best guess!

It's all In How You Manage the Events In Your Life

What I mean by this is simply you can make or break yourself. When unexpected things arise-and they will (Safeway had been here for over fifty years!) It's up to you to take control and take the next step. What is the next step? That will depend on your particular skills and talents and how you were brought up. While some of these decisions can be made over time-buying a house or car, others have to be made in an instant-life threatening or moral decisions. We were lucky in that we both had honest hard working parents-my dad was a used car salesman and Carole's dad was a policeman. Both of our mothers also worked. It goes back to being the best that you can be at whatever you do. You just get noticed and appreciated even though your supervisors and others don't tell you all the time.

Our Lucky Number Seven!

It was the summer of 1983. Carole had given me that smile again, Travis was on the way and would be here by Turkey Day!! Everything was going great. Chris had started school last fall and Eric would start in the fall-only three months from now.

Eric started school and Travis was born with no difficulties just like the other children. We had seven stockings to fill at Christmas time this year! We got them filled and it was really neat. At this point we knew we wanted more kids but we needed some time to adjust-the fact that I was working out of town a lot might have had something to do with this as well. Our next child wouldn't come for three years. One of the things we noticed was that it was impossible to find a baby sitter-actually about three kids ago! We never really had any great social agenda so it had little impact on us

When you have a large family the kids grow up in groups-three or so to a group. They hang out and play together, but still come to the aid of any brothers or sisters in time of need. Chris, Eric, and Todd played together and were constant companions. Chad, Becky, and Travis made up the next group. Katrina would sometimes play with the older boys, but, would also watch over the younger kids as well.

The other thing with a large family is that if you set a good example for the first few children, the rest will follow their example (hopefully!) We were very lucky in that our first children were very responsible almost from the time that they could walk or talk. I don't mean that they had jobs and bank accounts, but they would not leave the yard, would help clean up-putting their toys away, and would watch after each other. All of the other kids would follow suit in this fashion. It made life a lot easier for us.

Remember when I talked about the events in life that just "HAPPEN?"

The Van Tipped Over-What Happened To the Road!!?

Carole's parents had purchased an acreage up in a small Iowa town about an hour away. It was Saturday night and we were on our way to visit and spend the night. I was going to help Carole's father cut down some small trees and brush and put up a fence. It was about nine PM on a beautiful fall night and was already dark when we started out. We were in the family van which had seen better days but was still dependable. At this time Becky was five months old and Chris was almost seven years old. We were on a gravel country road when the road disappeared! What had actually happened was that there had been a lot of rain earlier in the week and part of the road had been washed out by a small drainage creek (usually!) that ran along the bottom of the road-about ten feet lower than the road. There were no street lights and it was so dark you couldn't see your hand in front of your face. We hit the washout and the van came to a very sudden stop. I realized that both of the right tires of the van were entirely off the road at that point. I was hoping that we could stay up on the road. No such luck! The van started sliding sideways off of the road into the ditch towards the creek. Nothing we could do! When the van had slid sideways far enough it started to roll-very gently as if God knew that we had small kids inside- it seemed like we were in slow motion as the van rolled over. We ended up on our top. We had five smaller children and a baby in the van along with a chainsaw and axe. We found all of the smaller kids and then we found Becky-crawling around on the ceiling of the van. It was just by an act of God that no one was hurt or killed for that matter.

We gathered everyone up and walked to a nearby farmhouse-Grandpa & Grandma's neighbors (in the country you can have neighbors that live a mile away?) They took us to the acreage where we spent the night. The next morning we inspected the van and the road to try to determine what had actually happened. In the day time you could clearly see that about one-third of the road had just washed away. They didn't put up barricades or anything like that in the country-you just had to know! As far as the van, it actually it didn't suffer too much damage. It was laying on it's top, with a dent in the roof and a cracked windshield. The neighbor whom had helped us the night before brought his tractor and we gently pulled the van back over onto it tires. After sitting on it's top all night some of the engine oil and transmission fluid leaked out. I refilled both of them and the van started right up-we ended up staying to help with the fence and actually drove the van home. Carole's parents followed us just to be sure we made it-and we did. Another family adventure with a happy ending!

Concussion Furniture

Back in the mid to late 70's there was a very popular type of rec-room furniture. We named it "Concussion Furniture" for good reason. The frames were made of 2x4's and 2x6's then stained-usually a darker tone. The cushions were large rectangular pillow types. These were very common-you have probably either seen or owned a set of these. They were extremely tough and would last forever. One day our oldest son Chris was playing hide and go seek in the family room when he slipped on the carpet hitting his head on one of the "Concussion" couches. Chris was a pretty sturdy boy (still is) but was no match for the "Concussion Couch". He received——you guessed it! A concussion. We actually just got rid of a similar set of these two years ago. Although it wasn't our original set, it was still true 70's vintage and had survived all those years. I'm sure that some of these still survive today-somewhere!

A Big Boom!!

We were awakened one winter night by a very big boom. It sounded like and explosion! Carole and I looked at each other in shock. I thought that the furnace or water heater had exploded. All of the kids that could walk came into our bedroom immediately. I checked the baby and the house. Everything seemed fine. We not only heard it but felt it as well. The sound and concussion had woke everyone up. All of the kids who could walk were instantly in our bedroom. I brought the baby into our room with Carole and the other kids then I went outside next as I didn't know if a neighbors house had blown up

Chapter III:
Challenge number two

No Job –Again!!!

I had been at the bread company for about two years now and had been a sales supervisor for the last year and a half. All was going great! Then; when you least expect it!We had a company meeting at Butternut Bread. The bakery had been sold to a competitor in our area who needed a high speed bakery as ours was-at least in 1984!

All of the management jobs would be lost-including mine. Starting over again!!

I had only been out of the grocery business for a couple of years and got right back into a management position with a local chain in a poorer part of Omaha. This was going to be fun!!I jumped right on in-kind of like going swimming with your clothes on! This job didn't pay as much as the sales supervisor role that I had at the bakery-at least to start. We had to sell our cabin on the river to help shore up our dwindling cash flow situation. We would regret this for years to come but nevertheless it was necessary.

I was working in a poorer community. It was a different world. Most of the people were great. They would bring us food from time to time-something that never happened anywhere else. I was an assistant manager to start. I would cash checks for people-just like at Safeway. I was also mostly working the night shifts-1-10 pm. At one time it had been a great high volume store, but that was many years ago. I made some hard decisions there and took some chances. I would carry my service revolver with me the first week of the month for the bank runs and deposits. A service revolver is a generic term for a large frame, large caliber pistol. Mine was a Smith & Wesson model 10 with a heavy barrel. The heavy barrel reduced the barrel jump and made it a pretty accurate gun, and if you run out of bullets it can be used as a billy club. I can still hit pretty good with it. I would also carry a smaller .22 caliber pistol in my boot as a back up. As I mentioned before I would only carry these when we had a lot of money around on the first of the month.

We got robbed the last week of the month in august of 1986. The robber bounded over the six foot booth enclosure like a gazelle! I still remember the incident to this day! I was talking very loud as to try to alert the checker that was working just outside of the office. It didn't work. She was so immersed in her work that she didn't hear anything except her customers. That is actually the way it should be! I tried to look at him to try to remember something about his appearance-clothing, facial features, hair color or style. He caught me trying to memorize his face. He was very angry-I'm surprised he didn't just shoot us right there! After robbing us he tried to get us to lie on the floor. My booth girl went right down, but I wouldn't. I figured that I had nothing to lose-when they have you lay on the floor with your face down they will sometimes shoot you and, I had already given him a reason not to have any witnesses.

It's very hard for anyone to shoot someone face to face, and that's just what I told him. "If you're going to shoot me you'll have to do it face to face." I really raised my voice that time! We argued for what seemed like about twenty minutes (in reality about thirty seconds) until a customer came in and scared him off. It was a pretty nerve racking experience. My booth girl had some medical problems after that and never came back to work full-time. From that point on I carried my gun to work every day. This was the first time I had been robbed, but would not be the last.

The robber was never caught. We found out who the police had suspected, but with only one witness they said they wouldn't prosecute. After that I never really felt at ease in that store-wonder why?!! Carole had always brought the kids to meet me at work periodically for lunch. Even with seven kids she would bring them. I just couldn't let her bring them down here.

We also had to deal with a lot of fights and disturbances in and around the store. I had played football and wrestled in high school, but, it had been fifteen years since then. The kids were asking about taking karate classes. We signed them up along with me. We took classes for about one year. The boys thoroughly enjoyed the classes and the whole martial arts ideology in general. In fact Eric did his forms (movements) for the talent show at his grade school. Everyone loved it, students and teachers alike!

I also benefited greatly from the karate classes. It was a great workout and I learned to better balance and control my body. It did come in handy more than once-a lot more!!

The kids were all doing well at this point. Chris, Eric, Todd, Katrina, and Chad were in school now. La Vista had a great public school system-and still does from what I have heard. While we lived in the suburbs the kids went to public schools and attended CCD classes (religion classes for Catholic children that go to public schools.)

The Crouses

Our neighborhood didn't really change too much for the first six or seven years. Then in 1986 my neighbor and friend that lived across the street (got me involved in the fire department) got transferred. He was in the military and it was his time to go. Later that year a new family moved onto the block. Dave and Shelly Crouse. Dave was also in the military. We really didn't get along from day one. They had two kids, a boy and a girl, and Shelly always looked like she had just come from a photo shoot. Our kids would play in the dirt and mud! She would make obnoxious comments to my wife and the kids. The one I remember the most was "Do you round your kids up on Saturday night to hose them down? It would be much faster than giving them all baths." We would get these kinds of comments all the time form other people and just laugh along. Her tone was very sarcastic and condescending. She did manage to influence a couple of the neighbors to join in with her at least somewhat. They would have a party or a barbecue in their driveway and every once in a while would stare at us or our kids who were just playing and having fun. When we would stare back Dave would come up and ask us why. When we told him he would pretend to tell his wife to stop staring and the rude comments, but, it never stopped until they left. But our kids still played with their kids-except for the Crouses' kids. The Crouse's kids never got dirty or played in the yard much that I can remember.

Shelley was just average looking until she put on her make up. She was a master of disguise! She could do wonders with a little face paint!

One day Shelly had pulled down to the cul de sac to turn around, she was taking the kids somewhere. She got a flat tire down there. It was in the morning and Dave was out of town that week. I was the only man around as I worked late that day. She asked me to change it for her and I did. I couldn't leave anyone in that position especially with kids in the car. As usual she was dressed to the hilt and her makeup was starting to run-it was summer and starting to get very warm by that time. As much as I wanted to just laugh at her I didn't. I changed her tire in record time. She thanked me and left. The next day she was back to her usual self. I remember my wife asking me if I would change her tire again if she needed help? I said yes. No more was ever said about it between us.

The Crouses would continue to be obnoxious and try to be somewhat disruptive to our family but, like all of the previous military people who lived in the neighborhood they were gone in three years. After they left I just couldn't look at those other neighbors who had joined in the ridiculing the same way. It would take a long time to get back to normal with them. We got along with all of the neighbors before they came, and most of them after they left. The bottom half of the cul de sac was a pretty close group.

That Special Smile

It was the late summer of 1985 when Carole gave me that special smile again-the one that comes right after a doctor visit. Kim was on the way. Kim was born in March of 1986. She was smaller than the rest of the kids And did not develop as fast. When it was time for her to start crawling she would scoot around on her back. We took her to the doctor and found that she had a hieatal hernia. She had the corrective surgery and it seemed to help. She still seemed to be behind the other children developmentally. We would soon find out why!

Holley is on the way

It was the spring of 1987 when Carole gave me that special smile again. Holley was on the way and would be here around Halloween. We would take turns taking the kids out trick-or-treating. Carole would take them to the immediate neighborhood then return home. If they wanted to go out farther (they always did!) I would take them into the surrounding areas. We would always stay within about six blocks of home as we knew most of the neighbors and the surroundings in those areas. Carole took the kids out that Halloween night (1987) but didn't get too far. She went into labor. Holley was born four minutes after midnight on November 1, 1987. If she had been born on Halloween we wouldn't have named her Holley. Who wants to be a Halloween baby named Holley? Holley came quick and was healthy just like most of the other kids-but with one exception. She couldn't handle dairy products. We had to buy her special soy based formula which she would require for the first year of her life. As a result, she didn't grow as fast as the other kids-at least at first (you should see her now-picture of health!) As a baby she was so small that one day one of Carole's sisters was over. Holley was standing very still at the far end of the couch. Holley moved abruptly and Carole's sister just about had a heart attack! She said she though that Holley was a doll-literally!!!

We had nine stockings to fill that Christmas! It was great! We drove older cars (we got rid of the new ones after the couple of years) and our house payment was cheaper than rent-it made it easier to financially survive. I would fix everything myself-no exceptions. I had learned these skills from our previous house. However, just in case I ran into something that I could not handle Carole's dad and brother, and brothers-in-law were there to help or give advice. I even put in a new furnace-saved over one-thousand dollars!

To achieve this task I bought a book on home improvement. It was the big yellow one. I still see these at garage sales every once in a while.

How do you transport a family of 11?

Just like our previous house, we had outgrown the family station wagon and the small van that we had been driving-both were also very tired! What next? The school system was having a sale on the used school busses and stretch vans that they used for student transportation. I stopped and checked them out. I put a bid in on two of the stretch vans-one blue and one red. We weren't quite ready for a real yellow school bus yet!

We got the two vans. The bodies weren't in the best of shape but they ran great. I was a pretty good mechanic but had only limited body and painting skills. I took a couple of courses at the local community college and ended up with sufficient skills to refurbish the vans. I did the red one first as it was for Carole. She would drive this for the next four years. It came out really neat and she would come to get a lot of compliments on it.

I drove the blue van. They both had enough seats for fifteen people. I fixed the body on my van but didn't make it as fancy as Carole's red van.

These would serve us well for the next four years. We would sell them for more than we had paid for them.

Abduction Attempt!

This is every parent's worst nightmare! To have your child abducted; the possibility that you will never see them again whether they are alive or dead-God forbid! It was the spring of 1988. Becky was in kindergarten at the grade school. She went in the mornings so when it was dismissal time Carole would meet her at the end of the school yard and walk her home. We only lived a block away from the school. On this particular day Becky wasn't there. Carole called her name out. We would later find that Becky had actually heard her mom calling her name, but was not allowed to answer. Even as a young girl Becky was very beautiful. She could have won any beauty contest she would have entered, but, we just weren't into that stuff.

As the minutes went by (seemed like hours!), Carole became more frantic.

She went up and talked to the principal and Becky's teacher at the school. One of the older kids who was on safety patrol that day said he saw Becky walking up the street (away from our house) with an older man. He said the man had a coat and a hat and that was all he remembered. Finally Becky came home crying . She said that a man had taken her as she walked right in front of the school. He had put his arm around her and "guided" her up the street away from school and our house. He told her about his kitchen with the yellow curtains and that she would like it. As they topped a hill they crossed the street into an undeveloped lot. At that point a lady at a nearby house stepped out onto her porch. Evidently the situation didn't look good to her. She startled the man who loosened his grip on Becky. At that point she was able to twist loose and run home. She was only three blocks from home at that point.

Becky made it home before the man could harm her. She would cry off and on for the rest of the afternoon. Carole also cried, especially when she found out the Becky had heard her mother calling her name. It's amazing at how bold pedophiles can be. As a result of that event Becky would never sleep downstairs again. We had a large family room in the walkout basement. On weekends or during the summers the kids would sleep down there instead of in their rooms. She was afraid that the man would come back for her.

We did contact the police. They investigated and did talk to the woman who saw Becky with the man. They never did find him. I don't know how hard they looked as when we suggested that they start watching the grade schools the police just kind of shrugged it off. It really didn't give us a great sense of security. Where were the AMBER ALERTS when we needed them?!

In any event we were very lucky and had narrowly escaped a horrific tragedy. Carole and I thanked God over and over again after that nearly catastrophic event. After that none of our kids left the school until they could see either Carole or myself-we still hold true to this today-at least for the smaller kids.

CHAPTER IV:
A HANDICAPPED CHILD

Challenge number 3:
Our First Special Needs Child

It was the winter of 1987-88. We started to notice that Kim was not acting like what we thought was quite normal. We had a fair amount of expertise by this time! Kim was kind of a puzzle to us. She seemed healthy but didn't develop as fast as the other kids. She would scoot around on her back instead of crawling-hernia related. She went from this to walking. She never did really crawl. Her speech seemed a little delayed too. It was when we went to a family Christmas Party, where there were other toddlers her age that our fears were confirmed. It was obvious that Kim was not developing like the other kids her age at the party. We took Kim to the Boystown National Hospital where they do a lot of research on pediatric disabilities. A pediatric neurologist saw Kim. It didn't take long for the doctor to figure out the problem. Kim has Rett's Syndrome.

It was March of 1988 and Carole and I were in the doctors office speechless at this point as the doctor explained the condition and what was known at that point and what was to be expected. Kim's prognosis wasn't good! Up until the late 70's or early 80's when a child was disabled they were thrown into a general diagnosis-Retardation. These kids (and adults) were just considered retarded, when, in reality they suffered from many different disorders.

Rett Syndrome was actually identified in 1966. Between then and about 1980 it was studied and then placed as a separate diagnosis. Very little was known about the disorder at that time. It was thought to be non-hereditary (something we would later find fault with!), and was a mutation of the X chromosome-MECP2.

The Bad News

The syndrome is a degenerative neurological disorder characterized by gradually losing what speech skills the girls had gained to begin with. They told us that Kim would be prone to seizures (very true) and was immediately put on anti-seizure medications. Rett's girls (notice I said girls) would also have great difficulty walking if they in fact ever started. The ones that did walk would usually be in a wheelchair by the time they were 8 years old. We were fortunate that Kim ever did walk. However, by this time she was walking on her toes-another sign that something is wrong. Kim was losing her ability to feed herself as well. They also told us that the life expectancy of Rett's girls is anywhere from eight-eighteen years. The girls wouldn't usually be taken by the disorder, but from a secondary medical condition. They can't tell us when they feel bad or what hurts. We just have to guess. The other way the girls pass on is from outside exposures such as walking through a window or falling from a deck. The doctor saw the concern in our faces and discussed several options, one of which was an institution. Carole and I looked at each other and we just knew inside that we could not put Kim in any kind of institution. We would care for her at home-she will remain part of our family.

That being said, the doctor told us right then and there that in a lot of cases a handicapped child leads to difficulty in the family unit. Many families with handicapped children end up in divorce from the sheer stress and strain it puts on them. For the next four years when we would bring Kim in for her quarterly checkups the doctor would ask how our family was handling the "extra burden?" If I would have to work on Kim's doctor day and could not be present the doctor would ask what happened to me? We assured the doctor that all was well-and it was!

The good News

Just what is Rett's Syndrome? It is basically a short circuit between the brain and the parts of your body that move-arms, legs, hands, and feet. The neurological pathways between these deteriorate over time. As they deteriorate the kids lose more and more of the every day functions that we all take for granted. Actually their brain is still very intact. Kim knows everything that is going on around her and knows who everyone is. She doesn't react as quickly as she used to. She will go to special needs schools for stimulation and socialization. You should have seen her at her senior prom! She was the Prom Queen.

When we got home with her we talked to the kids and explained as best we could Kim's situation. Our kids at that time ranged from two-twelve years of age. We knew we were going to need help as Kim couldn't dress herself, feed herself, and would never grow out of diapers. At this point Chris was almost thirteen and Eric was almost eleven. They would help feed Kim with Carole and I. We all took turns feeding Kim-boy could that girl eat!! As the kids grew older they would join in the "Feeding Schedule." All of our kids would share in this family tradition! Kim also liked being outside. We had a pretty big porch at the LaVista house. Kim would negotiate it well. She never fell off the side and when she came to the end she would come to an abrupt halt! She would just walk the porch for hours. Every once in a while she would stop and sit. She could still sit and get up on her own.

The disabilities put aside, Kim was and still is a very happy girl and is a joy to have around. She also was and still is a daddy's girl!! I tell her quite often "every dad should have a Kim" to appreciate the simple things in life, at which point she always gives me her big crooked smile and sometimes laughs out loud-she can still do that. She stares at you with her beaming eyes that are very hard to ignore. Kim makes up for what she can't do or say with her facial expressions and what hand and body movements she can still manage.

Kimberley Willits

There are trade-offs in life. We often work hard, looking forward to some recreation that we thoroughly enjoy whether it be camping, fishing, hiking, or any number of physical or non-physical activities or hobbies that make it all worth while for us. As long as we have that balance we are living a great life and look forward to those times we spend with friends, family, and then just doing those things that make us happy.

The one thing above all that we must not forget is how to laugh. I read somewhere that everyone should laugh (from the belly-no cheating cheek laughs!) at least five times a day. I just laughed a big belly laugh at one of the emails one of my kids sent to me. That's ok. Email laughs count as long as they are belly laughs. A parting thought. Anyone involved in this process must always not forget to laugh-or how to laugh! Under these circumstances especially too much negative feelings and emotions can definitely do you in (along with anyone close to you!)

I Tease You Because I Love You!

From time to time I have to admit that have I teased my kids. They would say something like I'm tired or I'm thirsty. My response to that would be "I'm Dad. Glad to know you thirsty!" They would try not to laugh and could sometimes hold it for a while but it usually it would sneak out. When they would be in a bad mood I would say "I'll bet you can't laugh by the time I count to 3. 1, 2, 2 ½, 2 ¾, 2 17/18ths, 2 55/56ths, and so on." I never got to 3 until they were laughing-which usually didn't take too long. When they would ask why we teased them so much we would say "I tease you because I love you!"

It's Every Father's God-Given Right to Tease His Children!

This was my other comeback when my kids asked about teasing. I would say "It's every father's God-given right to tease his children!" From this response I would always get obnoxious looks-eye rolling, frowns (didn't last too long or it was known that we'd go right into the "Can't laugh by 3 routine!", etc, etc. Once in a while I would get a somewhat serious objection to the above at which I would say "I'm just trying to build your character". It truly does!

First child in Junior High!

By this time Chris was in junior high school and Eric was in sixth grade. Along with Todd, they were definitely a force to be reckoned with. I had been a

34

wrestler in high school, and from the time they started walking, I had wrestled around the house and yard with them. They picked it right up! They would wrestle with the neighborhood kids and always come out victorious. This along with the martial arts training made them a very formidable opponent. Even the kids that were two to three years older would not wrestle Eric after a while as they knew what the outcome would be and didn't want to be embarrassed. All three would wrestle in junior high and Eric would go on to be a champion wrestler in high school. He won almost every tournament he entered-not bad for a kid with the nickname "Rabbit!"

One day Carole and I were sitting on the front porch when Chris, Eric, and one of their friends from down the street came home from Junior high. Within a minute or two a car came speeding down the street and stopped in front of our house. Six teenagers jumped out and wanted to fight the boys. I guess one of our boys had been talking to a girl that one of these kids liked and it didn't set to well with them. They had the boys out numbered two to one, and had a size and age advantage as well. I intervened to try to get to the bottom of the dispute. It looked to me like they were just trying to pick a fight that they had overwhelming odds of winning . I asked the teenagers what their main concern was and they said that one of our boys had said something inappropriate to the girl in question. I looked at our kids and angrily ordered them into the house for further "discipline." The other kids got into their car and left.

Once they were inside the house and the situation had been defused I told them that I didn't mean anything that I had said to them and that that was the only way that I could end the confrontation without further physical action. They were all very relieved that it ended peacefully. We never saw the other kids again.

Community Moped

We were at a garage sale one day and spotted a moped that was for sale with a very reasonable price tag. It started right up so we purchased it and rode it home (home was only 3 blocks away.) From that point on it was known as the community moped. Everyone in our family as well as most of the neighbor kids rode it. I didn't do anything to that moped. It ran for two or three years (I forget) until it finally died. We definitely got our fifty bucks out of that! In today's world the liability issues alone would have made this impossible to do. I guess they just don't make them like they used to!

A Near tragedy!

When the kids would go up to the convenient store they would go through the back yard and cut across the big open field out back. By now there were plans to make a golf course. Grading had already started. The plans also called for several small ponds. The grading crew had already dug a deep hole for the first pond. It was very deep-ten to twelve feet deep. We had gotten a lot of rain the last week or so. When the kids decided to go to the convenient store they took Holley with them. Holley was only two and a half years old at this point and very small. She did however have very good balance and could walk great. On the way back home she got a little too close to the edge of the pond. It was still muddy at the edge. The edge of the bank gave way and she just slipped right in the pond. Todd had seen this and dove in (fully clothed) after her. She could not be seen in the dark murky water, however, Todd found her and brought her back to the edge of the pond where Chris and Eric helped pull her onto dry land. Everyone was shaken up over this as were Carole and I. Todd was not only the hero of the day, but the hero of the year as far as we were concerned. From that day on we wouldn't let the kids take that route to the convenient store any more. We really didn't get any arguments from them.

We All Lose Focus At Times

We had a couple of months that were particularly stressful. Money was very short and the children were getting older, growing like weeds, and eating like horses! It was a battle just to keep food on the table. At the time I was an assistant manager for a large local food retailer. My earnings were just average.

I had been less than happy for a couple of weeks in a row (I broke one of my cardinal rules.)Carole and the kids had noticed from the start. They kept trying to cheer me up but I guess I wasn't coming around. One day Carole had just had enough of my poor attitude. She had all of the kids come in and line up sitting on the couch or couches as at that time we had nine kids and it took the two large couches to seat all of them. She looked at me with disgust in her eyes and said "Okay. Who do you want to send back?!!" I just looked at her-my mouth must have fallen open almost to the floor. I asked her to repeat her question. She said "If you want to send someone back do it now!" I felt stupid. She said "we'll get through this. We always do. You are in good health, the kids were in good health. Why are you feeling so sorry for yourself?!" The kids didn't really understand what she was getting at and

I was glad. I remember Katrina was laughing and teasing one of the smaller children at the time-a true Willits!

I really felt stupid at this point. I apologized to my wife and all of the kids.I readjusted my attitude that evening. She was right. They were all right! I had so much more to be thankful for than the average bear. We did get through that tough time and all of the others that would come along as well!

We all sometimes lose our focus on our particular mission. Whether we are raising a family, running a business, or just trying to survive we need to keep our eyes on our objectives and take the path or paths that will help us to see our ambitions through. I lost mine for a while but, thanks to the help of my wife, I found it again. I'm not going to say that I never had any more bad-attitude days or that I didn't lose my focus at times, but if and when I did, I did regain it a lot quicker-Carole has never had to line up the kids again. It would almost be impossible at this point!

That Special Smile and My Verification Technique!

It was between Thanksgiving and Christmas of 1988 when Carole gave me that special smile. Whenever she gave me that special smile I would confirm it by feeling her abdominal area. I had learned through ny EMT courses at the Volunteer Fire Department that during pregnancy the abdominal muscles tighten up somewhere between one to three months. If her muscles were starting to tighten up I knew she was pregnant-it never failed! Melodey was on the way. By that time I had changed jobs from managing a store in northeast Omaha to being a manager for a larger local chain retail grocer. They didn't have any stores in the poorer parts of Omaha so it was a change. I didn't have to carry a gun to work! I had trained at one of their west Omaha stores and was transferred to a south Omaha location. We were back on track as the job move also meant a better salary.

CHAPTER V:
MELODEY

Melodey

Melodey was a very difficult delivery. It was the spring of 1989. She decided at the last minute she didn't want to come out and meet her brothers and sisters, mom, and dad, and everyone else who were patiently (or impatiently) awaiting her arrival! The doctor actually had to go in and was pulling her by her head-very hard! He had one foot on the ground and one foot on the edge of the delivery table for leverage! I was sure her neck would be broken and yelled at the doctor "you're going to pull her head off!" They told me to sit down and remain quiet or I'd be removed from the delivery room. When she finally emerged we discovered that the umbilical cord was wrapped around her waist. It's a miracle that she survived at all!Carole suffered from this delivery far more than any of the others as well. Her insides suffered multiple injuries. After the event one of the attending nurses told us that the doctor should have performed a C-section and that we should consider a lawsuit. We talked about a lawsuit but decided not to pursue one. Melodey stopped breathing the first night and would spend the next three days in the Newborn Intensive Care Unit. Carole had to stay in the hospital a couple of extra days as well. They ended up going home together after a seven day hospital stay. When they came home Melodey came home with some new hardware-an apnea monitor. This was new to us at that point, but we would get plenty of experience with these as time went on-definitely not a good thing! We learned how to "belt her up" every night and during naps. The sound of those apnea alarms was ear piercing-it had to be. It had to be able to wake you up from a sound sleep and it definitely did the job! We would have to go into her room on many occasions to gently jostle her just enough to get her back on track breathing normally again. We were learning a new normalcy that would follow us through all of the years-and still does!

Carole had healed fully and we were getting back to our regular routine when in October of that year Carole gave me that special smile-again! I felt her stomach to confirm (or dismiss) the upcoming event. It was definitely upcoming! This time it was twins! All was going well and we were getting used to our new routine (apnea monitor stayed with Melodey and us) when in December of 1989 Melodey got very sick. She had constant severe diahria for a day and became lethargic. We took her to the emergency room where she was immediately admitted to the Pediatric Intensive Care unit. It took her two weeks to get well enough to come home. She was diagnosed with a severe blood infection. It had a name-one of those long ones that I can't remember. This was right before Christmas 1989, Carole stayed up with her at the hospital day and night as she would with all of the kids when they were in the hospital. It was after Melodey came home that Carole had a miscarriage and lost the twins. It was Christmas day 1989 and was the saddest day of out married lives.

It was the next spring that Carole once again had that special doctor's appointment accompanied by that special smile. Michelle was on the way! We now had ten children with one more on the way which would make 11. We had outgrown our second house! We started looking at larger homes. We had two choices; either a newer area with large homes (way too expensive for us) or returning to the older neighborhoods in central or south Omaha. That seemed more realistic. The houses were built to last and had plenty of room for larger families.

Challenge Number 4 Tragedy!!

We were busy remodeling our house to get it ready to sell. Melodey, the baby that we had been through so much with died in what seemed at the time to be a tragic home accident. You can never really know what it's like to lose a child until it happens to you. She lingered in the hospital for a day before she died. We kept thinking that this was just a bad dream and that we would wake up to find Melodey sleeping in her crib. I'm not going to go into details on this as it is still very painful. We would later find out that she probably had a disorder or disorders that contributed to her death. As parents you still grieve.

I had never had to make funeral arrangements before or even been close to any such situation and was not in any condition to do so. I had been crying in Melodey's room on the day I was to make the funeral arrangements and it was pretty evident. Thankfully, Carole's father stepped up and was there to guide me through this process. He seemed to always be there at our times of need. Melodey had a very nice funeral that had an overflow crowd. I took several weeks off of work. Carole took several months off work.

The support from our families, friends, co-workers, and the community in general was just tremendous. We received sympathy calls and cards from people that we hadn't seen or talked to in years.

You never really get over the loss of your child. The only thing that helps is time. The thing is that it is so unnatural. Children are supposed to bury their parents, not the other way around. We still count Melodey as one of our children-she is. She just isn't here with us. Instead she is up in heaven watching over us.

Michelle was born on Travis' birthday in November. Travis called her his birthday present. He still does! She was a normal delivery and progressed well, however, she would have some underlying learning disabilities that we had never dealt with before.It would be a new learning experience for us.

The Victorian Mansion!!

That next spring we bought an old Victorian mansion in an older part of town. It was a fixer-upper just like our first house-more or less. More, because there was a lot more of it. Three floors and a full basement. Less because it didn't need a total rebuild like the first house. It would take me and the kids (by now I was including the older kids in some of the renovations) almost ten years to complete this task. We did have some distractions and interruptions though-sometimes life just has a habit of getting in the way!

That being said we came upon this house by sheer coincidence. I had bought a set of used tires from an old friend. After I paid him he asked "is there anything else I can do for you?" I then proceeded to ask him if he knew of any big old houses for sale-not really expecting a positive response! He looked at me kind of funny and said that he just might. A distant relative of his was trying to sell a large old house that they had owned. It was a mess. They had raised 12 children there and had tried to keep it up, but, it had not been inhabited for the last six or seven years. He really couldn't list it through a real estate agency as it was in too poor condition. It pretty much had to be a cash or almost cash sale. We got our house ready to sell and we cleared almost enough to buy it. The rest we got on a mortgage from our bank. We proceeded to start our second fixer-upper project and the rest is history!

I broke one of my cardinal rules with this house. We hired a contractor to help with the repairs. There was just so much that needed to be done it seemed like the thing to do. He was doing some work on the house next door and did a very good job. We checked him out and found that he had been in business for over twenty years. He also checked out great with the Better Business Bureau. He did great starting out, but, when we got ahead on payments he disappeared. We did find him after a couple of weeks. He was always going to come back and finish, but never did. We filed a case in small claims court, but, later found out that he had filed bankruptcy. At that point a suit was useless. We lost about fifteen hundred dollars on the deal. Lesson learned! Thank God we hadn't paid him all of the money up front. We would still farm out some of the small projects, but we never paid until the job was complete and to our liking.

The three largest areas that needed repair on this house were the balcony which needed to be rebuilt, exterior painting of the entire house, and the lawn and yard was an absolute mess. We did the yard and lawn first. It required a retaining wall along the driveway. We put in a tie wall. We added steps in two places, a large set that was eight feet wide, and a small set that was thirty inches wide.

Next we rebuilt the balcony. We had to replace the flooring and some of the rafters underneath to get enough support. Next we built a railing that matched the period of the house. We then put in a floor/roof combination of hard rubber. It sealed very well and wasn't that hard.

Painting was a different story. It hadn't had a good painting for probably fifty years or more. I mean the kind where you really scrape and replace any bad wood that you find. We did find a lot of bad wood too! We changed the color from white to a medium blue. We went as fast as we could but being a working family and the house being so large, it took almost a year to do the job right. In the meantime the city inspectors came around and tagged the house. They said it needed painting. It was half white and half blue. The scaffolding was still up when they cited us. We were supposed to have the house done by January. I didn't plan on painting during the winter (you really can't paint outside in Nebraska in the winter months.) I went down to city hall to try to straighten this out. They wouldn't budge. I argued that I was in the process of painting the house when they said that I need to paint the house. It sounded ludicrous to me. They gave me a ninety day extension and we got it finished in that time. You talk about a cluster! This was it!

This house did have many redeeming features though. It had breathtaking natural woodwork throughout the main floor, original dark oak wood floors throughout, four fireplaces, a ten foot high stained glass window, six bedrooms on the second floor, and servant's quarters on the third floor. The third floor was set up into two separate apartments. The first was a studio apartment that may have housed a single person, and the second was a larger room maybe for a man & wife. It also had, at one time anyway, a coal stove for heat and cooking. The third floor also had hidden passageways that, we were told, were used during the prohibition days to hide certain illegal activities. We found out that when we were looking for one of the kids they would not be found unless they wanted to be, or, we were smart enough not to call their name until we were close enough to see them. With all of the rooms and passageways they could easily avoid us and did on more than one occasion!

This had been a very grand house at one time and would be again with a lot of work, materials, and know how! The house was built by a successful businessman in the very late 1800's. It had been passed through several owners along the way ending up as a boarding house for college students. The latter is what took a big toll on the house. As bad as it looked it was still structurally sound. At one time it had gas lights throughout. Some of the fixtures are still there. It also has a hand water pump in the basement. These older houses sometimes would have cisterns (underground pools to catch the rainwater runoff.) They would use this water for washing clothes and cleaning as it was very soft water-you don't need a water softener!

I took us nearly ten years to get this house to where it was comfortable and looking good. You notice I didn't say "done." It seems like you are really never done with a house. There is always something that you want to change or upgrade. This house had a large walk in entry hall with tiger maple paneling. It had a cove with coat and hat racks as well as a walk in closet for more weather gear storage.

Just to the left of the entry hall are a set of pocket doors leading to the parlor. The parlor has it's own fireplace which is highly carved and finished in dark cherry wood. It also has a large beveled mirror on top of the mantle. There are pocket doors leading to the library.

At the end of the entry hall some twenty feet from the front door is the door to the dining room. The dining room is rather plain compared to the rest of the house. The only extra feature it had was a china cabinet built above the large radiator. The entire first floor of the house has designs stenciled into the plaster from the floor to the ceiling. I have never seen anything like it before or after we lived there, even in the fancier houses that we had been to.

The library was just that. It had book shelves on both sides of the fireplace that filled in the rest of the west wall of that room. The library was eighteen feet long. The fireplace was just like the one in the parlor. This one was mahogany with designs carved into the wood. We filled up one side of the bookshelves with books and put pictures on the other side.

The kitchen was a disaster when we first bought the house. There at one time had been a set of stairs going down to the basement from the kitchen but they had been taken out. To get to the basement you had to go outside and in the side basement door in the driveway. This was always fun in the winter time! I remodeled the kitchen myself and put a trap door in the floor that would open up to a set of stairs to access the basement. We also added on a side deck and a back porch. The back porch would have a handicapped lift for the handicapped kids. The kitchen also has it's own fireplace that was once used for cooking and for warmth.

The stairs up to the second floor were as grand as ever! There was a landing half way up and on the landing was a ten foot high stained glass window. At the top of the staircase was the master bedroom and dressing room. The master bedroom has a fireplace. Just outside the front windows of the master bedroom is the balcony. The balcony runs the full front width of the house and then runs along the south side for about fifteen feet. We had to rebuild this but, once it was done was well worth the effort. We would sit out on the balcony and have a very good vantage point of the neighborhood.

Sometimes the kids would sleep out on the balcony.

The second floor bathroom was in marble tile. The entire floor and walls up to the five foot level was covered in white marble. It still had the old pull chain toilet with the wooden tank overhead. The sink was carved marble with chrome over brass fixtures. No expense was spared when this house was built.

The Victorian Mansion

We Are Not Alone!!!

We had a different experience in this house-one we had never had before. We soon discovered that we were not alone in the house. As I started the repair process We found that there were SPIRITS sharing our house with us. I was never one to believe in such things. If I couldn't hold it, it didn't exist as far as I was concerned. Carole and the kids tried to tell me for some time about our "guests". I wasn't having any of it. It took an encounter of my own-an unmistakable one to convince me.

Some people don't believe in spirits (like me) until they confront you, as happened to me. We had several psychics (including the police psychic) survey the house. They all said the same thing. "You have several spirits in your house with you".

Batman!!

At first our Victorian mansion didn't have storm windows or screens. We measured all of the windows and ordered thirty two storm windows with screens. The house also didn't have air conditioning which made for some very uncomfortable nights while trying to sleep. The older kids slept up on the third floor and would leave the windows open at night. This only went on for a couple of weeks until the storms arrived. However, in this time a number of bats flew in and took refuge in the very top of the loft which was actually equivalent to a fourth floor.

At first we couldn't understand how the bats were getting into the house. From time to time we would find them in one of the bedrooms or in a hallway. We would wake up in the middle of the night to a loud fluttering sound, almost a high pitched squeak. It was a bat flying around. I used a fishing net to catch them. It actually worked great. I got to where I could catch them on the first swing. It was kind of like those big fat plastic waffle bats that you use to hit the small waffle balls! Once they were in the net they would freeze up or go into shock. I would just place the whole net outside and leave it till morning. The bats were always gone in the morning. This ritual went on for five or six years. I didn't know there were that many bats in the city!

Our Parish Priest

I really haven't mentioned too much about religion. When we lived in the suburbs we were fairly active in the church. We weren't the family that attends every mass or anything like that. We just believed that we should contribute to the parish in time and effort as well as financially. One of my contributions was to help organize an effort to finance the building of a new church. The parish had been around for more than 100 years and had outgrown the tiny church that had been there almost as long. I was asked to help organize a grass roots effort to build a new church. It was going to be quite costly, but would be worth every penny in the end. The campaign was successful and the new church was built. The new church was dedicated in 1982.

Father Steinbrenner was instrumental in the building of the church as well as a good friend of our family. He would take the boys to sports events if they were a one day drive or less and many college level games. He even took me to the Notre Dame-Boston College Football game in 1992.

I had never been to Notre Dame. Once we entered the campus there was just an aura of fraternal brotherhood and friendship. Even though Boston College was a heavy favorite that day, I knew that Notre dame was going to win. They did. In grand style! Boston College didn't even score until the second and third teams for Notre Dame were on the field. It was a trip I'll remember for the rest of my life! Father Steinbrenner passed away early in 1993. Our family lost a great friend with his passing.

We were now back at Our Lady of Lourdes, the same parish Carole and I were married in and where Chris and I were baptized together. I would go on to be active in the parish helping to coach my daughter's soccer teams and contributing financially as well as time and effort to certain parish events and activities.

Snake In The Grass

One thing that we had noticed since we moved back to the older part of town is that there is a very good supply of garter snakes ever present. These range anywhere from six inches to three feet long. They can't really bite you although they do try. Some of the kids loved to catch them and "show them off" to Carole and myself. They never really wanted to keep these as pets or anything thank god! This went on the whole time that we lived at the house on thirtieth ave-fifteen years! The kids would become pretty good snake tamers and trainers. I'm sure that the snakes didn't share this opinion though! We also had our share of opossums and raccoons while we were there.

There was also a family of raccoons living in the house next door for a while. The house next door had stood vacant for several years and had some holes in the eaves and roof. The raccoons would climb right in and come back out after dark. We watched them come out one at a time one night and counted them. There was nine of them. There was a father, a mother, and seven smaller raccoons. We could see their heads pop up above the roof line

Chapter VI:
The Next Set of Children

Alex Is On The Way

Guess what? Carole had another doctor's appointment. And guess what? You guessed it! Alex would be here some time in early January of 1992. We had spent the rest of 1991 getting the "NEW" house just to be livable.

We were back in Omaha and had decided that the children should go to catholic schools-at least for grade school. I had been a convert to Catholicism. I took the classes after we were married. Chris and I were baptized at the same ceremony in 1976 at Our Lady of Lourdes.

I had never attended a Catholic school but instead had gone through the public school system. Carole had actually graduated from Our Lady of Lourdes. We wanted more for our children. It's normal for a parent to want a better life for his children than they had. So far we have been able to provide that.

Chad would be the first Willits child to graduate from Our Lady of Lourdes Catholic School-but far from the last! Chad started OLL on the fall of 1991. We have had children there ever since and still do! Kaylee will graduate from OLL in the spring of 2012. Twenty-one years of attendance by our family-most of those years we had multiple children there. Sometimes we had five children attending at the same time. For high school the kids went to Central High in Omaha. It is probably the best high school, at least academically, in the state. We will have the same type of attendance longevity there as well. I actually graduated from Central High School in Omaha in 1971.

Christmas in the new house was great. We had more room then we had ever had before-you notice that I didn't say "more than we knew what to do with!" It didn't take us long to "spread out". Some of the kids still had to share rooms, but the rooms were bigger. We put Chris, Eric, and Todd on the third floor. They had basically their own apartments up there.

When we would have get-togethers at the house we could hold more people than the outside parking could accommodate. This was a family house, a banquet hall, and a limitless play area all-in-one.

Alex was born on January 9th, 1992. I have stated before that all of our kids were either blond haired and blue eyed or brown hair and brown eyed with a darker complexion. Alex was blond haired and brown eyed and still is.

The spring of 1992 brought several new experiences to our family. First and foremost, Chris, our oldest son, started driving. Chris was a very good driver. In fact he would kind of let his guard down a little because he had mastered the art of driving (or so he thought!) He would go on to have several scrapes, but nothing serious.

The Willits "Cowboys" Alex, Robert, Veronica. And Michelle.

How do you Handle so Many Children Especially When They Start Driving ?

We took the common sense approach.We would supply their basic needs-food, housing, and clothes, and toys, hobbies club memberships etc. When they grew to want more such as designer clothes, cars, cell phones-or pagers (at that time), they would get a job and pay for these non-necessities them selves. This still holds true today for our children.

In Looking back, all of our children had a job by the time they were sixteen (most were younger!) A lot of the kids had paper routes before they got real jobs-anywhere from ten-fourteen years old. From 1987 till 2007 I would get up at 4:30 AM on Sundays to "assist" the kids with their routes. That is just too early to send them out alone. My dad did the same for me! I would get a few breaks in there from time to time. One of the kids wouldn't want a paper route (OH BOY!) Another tradition or rule was when you get a job, you have to open a bank account (savings). I feel it helps to teach the kids responsibility both morally and financially.

The kids would pay for their own cars-not only the purchase price, but, all of the costs associated with driving. They pay for their own insurance, gas, and upkeep (parts only-I supply the labor) A final thought on this is that when your children start driving it is most important that you don't forget to laugh!

We Are Parents All of Our lives!

Once we have children we are parents all of our lives. Later on we may be grandparents as well as parents. When you become a parent you automatically sign up for the possibility of grandparenthood and welcome it if it comes!

When we go through the parenting process we see our roles as parents change from absolute dictators (birth to teen years), to guidance counselors (teen years to early adults), and to very interested observers (adult years). Every once in a while we may slip back into one of the other roles to help our kids, but hopefully, it will only be temporary. And last but not least, don't forget to laugh!

I'll Scratch Your Back For a Dollar!

This was a ritual that took place at our house from the time that our first son, Chris, was old enough to go to the kwik shop by himself (it was only on the other side of the field). The kids would take turns at this after I got home from work. They would go up to the kwik shop and buy a pop and at the beginning they would have enough left over for some candy. The time required to earn the dollar started out at one hour and through the years has dwindled down to 10 minutes-the law of supply and demand strikes again! After a while I would buy enough pop to last most of the week. We have always kept two refrigerators-still do, and we would use one for the milk, pop, and juices. Instead of giving them a dollar I would just give them a pop. To get pop and or treats the children would have to ask or earn them.

Career Change

I had been in retail grocery management for almost twenty years at this point and was ready for a change. There had been some changes in the grocery workplace as well, through the years. The employees working in the stores were making much less than ten years ago-a little more than half what they made before.

You've heard of trickle-down effect? Have you ever heard of the trickle-up effect? We found out the hard way about this one. Through the years whenever the employees would get raises, management would automatically get raises to keep their wages above the employees. The retail unions had been broken over the last ten years when the only two large union grocery companies in town, had just closed up and left-Safeway and Hinky-Dinky (started out life as Piggly Wiggly back in the 1930's) The wage scales for employees had reversed to the point that the wage scales for management was also affected. I was running a large volume supermarket making about the same as when I was a second assistant fifteen years earlier. It was time to re-evaluate!

As I had mentioned before I grew up in the auto industry and learned a lot about auto repair. I had kept up with the changes over the years. I would buy cars that didn't run or were wrecked (but not totaled) and do what ever it took to get them back on the road. Sometimes it was simple, sometimes I had to rebuild the entire drive train! The positive things that this did for us is to supply an inexpensive means of dependable transportation for our family, and to keep the costs way down-necessity with a large family! It also kept me in practice.

Our friends and neighbors saw what I was doing with the cars and trucks and were always asking me to help them with theirs. I started doing this part time and within a couple of years had enough business to open a shop of my own. Along the way I had picked up some commercial customers and would service their fleets and employees cars as well.

By this time I had some of the older boys helping me. Chris, Eric, and Todd picked the mechanics up very well. Chris actually could rebuild engines and help with transmissions and clutches. I bought my own tow truck and was able to tow customers' vehicles as necessary. We would continue to have a successful repair business for the next six years. I would have to close this not for lack of business, but a specific chain of events which would come up would force me to make a change. Sometimes life has a funny way of sneaking up on you!

That Special Smile

Guess what? You guessed! Carole had another doctor's appointment. Robert was on the way. He would be here in the early spring of 1993. We had already worn a path in the road from the "new" house to the delivery room. I could see the ruts in the street! (not really-it just seemed that way.) The new house was coming along and was looking better every day. When the kids would bring their friends home their friends would be amazed at the inside-the outside still needed work.

Robert was born in March of 1993. We named him Robert after my brother Bob. By the time Robert was six months old Carole had been to the doctor again. I'm not even going to say it this time.

The Tent Burned Down!!

About this time Travis was becoming interested in scouting. He became a cub scout. We had a pretty close knit group with the scouts and their parents. We went camping a lot. On one of the camping trips the camp stove that I brought (wouldn't you know it!) flared up out of control and burned down one of the tents! How do you fix that?! We cleaned it up as best we could but it was a total loss! I apologized to the tents owners (thanks God they weren't in the tent!) They understood accidents happen-having kids tends to help with that mindset. I replaced the tent. At that time money was a bit tight so it took several months to save up enough extra money for the new tent.

We have remained friends and still are to this day. YES. We did go on more camping trips together. I, however, wasn't allowed to cook. I couldn't understand why-maybe they don't like my cooking?! Oh well!

Chad Gets Hit By a Car

We got a call early one evening that Chad had been hit by a car. The call was from a police officer and the officer let us know that Chad seemed to be alright. We 4rushed right down to the scene. The incident took place about four blocks from our house. Chad had been riding a bicycle down a hill when his brakes just quit working. He rolled through a stop sign and was struck by a car. Chad landed on top of the hood of the car and rolled off into the grass parking area between the street and the sidewalk. He narrowly missed a telephone pole which was just to the left of him.

When we got there Chad was moving around and seemed to be fine, although his forehead was covered with blood. We took him to the emergency room to have the cut evaluated and dressed. We wanted to make sure he had not sustained a more severe head injury. Sometimes it is very hard to tell.

The bicycle was totaled and the car had also sustained a fair amount of damage. Before we were through we would replace the hood and windshield on the car. That's ok in my book because some things or people just can't be replaced. We were lucky this time. When we got home we checked the brakes on all of the bikes. We had five or six at the time. We found one other with what I would consider substandard brakes. We fixed that one immediately.

We would tease Chad from time to time about having been hit by a car and the car getting the worse of the injury or damage in that case! However, we knew in our hearts and still know to this day just how lucky we all were that evening.

Veronica is on the Way!!

Veronica was born in June of 1994. She also was a very healthy baby. The Victorian Mansion was starting to fill up! When we decided to buy this house one of the factors that we considered was future use. As the children grew older and left home we would close off the third floor as bedrooms. Our plan was to make these guest rooms. We figured that the kids would get married and may move away to different cities. The third floor was actually large enough to put up two families if the kids would want to come back-say during the holidays or for special events. We never got to use this plan because none of the kids have moved out of state-or even town, at least for good, at least at this time!

By this time Carole was working at a hospital-guess where? In the newborn nursery! If the shoe fits! I guess it fit because by the time Veronica was nine months old we had another announcement. Cole was on the way!

By this time Eric had been working for two years and had saved up enough to buy a car. Eric was the most sensible, considerate, and modest teenager you'll ever meet. This along with his future accomplishments would carry him far-literally. Chris and Eric were both driving now. That meant that they didn't need rides anymore and actually took some of the pressure off of Carole and myself by taking the other kids the places they need to go. At times it would seem like in our off-work times all we did was chauffer the kids around. School activities, sports, part time jobs, movies, and other social activities kept not only the kids, but Carole and I very busy.

When your kids start driving it is kind of a bitter sweet emotional state. You are happy that they are being responsible enough to drive and have mastered the skills necessary to handle a car. None of our kids started out driving anything other than a car. The trucks and suv's would come later, after they had some "street sense". Also, you are not their personal chauffer and can devote more time to other things which may have been greatly neglected.

However, there is definitely a trade off with this. Just as you are not obligated to transport them around, you are equally nervous every time they come home a little late or the phone rings unexpectedly. I was never a great drinker, but every now and then I would just like to sit down and have a beer or two. I found this to be very hard to do when the kids were out driving. If something happened I didn't want to show up at the scene smelling like alcohol.

The kids did have some minor accidents and traffic infractions. However, none of them totaled their car or anyone else's vehicle. No other drivers or pedestrians were injured as a result of our children driving. The only car that was totaled was done as a result of another driver's negligence. He is the one who tried to blame one of our sons for the deed. He would go on to lose his case in court. It was just too bad it had to go that far. It would have been much cheaper and easier to just pay him off. We had to hire a lawyer and an engineer to prove our case. We just felt that that would be like admitting to something our son didn't do just to grease the wheels of the court system and the other guy's hands!

When the children did have traffic accidents they had to save up for the parts to fix the cars themselves. I would do the labor and painting but usually had them assist in the repairs. If their insurance went up they would have to cover that as well. They would have to take full responsibility for their actions while driving. This would seem to be a bit hard at the time, but it got them used to the real world.

Some of their school friends were driving around new or newer cars that had been purchased by their parents. Our children were just as proud of their older (sometimes looked it) cars because they had earned the money to purchase these all by themselves.

Vacation In The Rockies!

Some friends of ours had a cabin in the Rocky Mountains. They offered it to us if we wanted to take our family vacation there. We welcomed the opportunity with open arms. It was our first visit to this beautiful part of the country. The ride there took ten hours. We stopped and camped at Medicine Bow National Park in Wyoming the first night. That in itself was beautiful with the mountains and colorful forests. We brought a large tent and sleeping bags for all of us. I wouldn't have minded staying here for the entire week.

We left early the next morning and headed south through Denver. I couldn't believe the traffic on the freeways in Denver! I though that Omaha was bad at the time-not any more! The cabin was just south of Colorado Springs. It took us about 3 hours to get there. As we got closer to the cabin we noticed two things. Number one was that the terrain was becoming red and dusty. Number two was that we were gradually rising in elevation. Their cabin was actually near the top of one of the mountain ranges.

When we arrived at the cabin it was the most beautiful and secluded spot I had ever seen. The cabin itself was an A-frame. Outside the cabin-and I mean right outside, there was a small mountain lake-or pond. It was about half the size of a football field but looked pretty deep. Our friends said there were fish in the lake and it was okay to go fishing. We brought poles and guess what? Our friends were right! We caught twelve mountain trout.We had dinner! I cooked the trout over an open fire and they were great! Whatever the kids couldn't finish I did-to the point that I got an upset stomach! You know what they say bout too much of a good thing? I found out the hard way!

While in the area we visited the local tourist attractions one of which is Pike's Peak. We drove up to the top of the mountain. The view was breathtaking! The other thing was that it was snowing at the top! It was the middle of July and we had actually been wearing tank tops and tee shirts (and were still sweating) when we started the drive up-took about an hour. Somewhere along the way (about half way up) I had to turn on the heater.

We stayed there for four days and nights and when it was time to leave we were refreshed and ready to tackle the world again. The mountain cabin was isolated form the outside world-no television and it was hard getting radio reception up there as well as we were between mountain peaks. There was nothing to remind us of the stresses of the outside world.

We headed home straight east through Kansas. Right about at the center of the state we heard a loud POOF! We had blown a tire. It was really blown and not repairable. We had a spare and put it on. We were back on our way home as we passed the next larger town we stopped and got the blown tire replaced-good thing as we would later find out! We took the highways back home as I didn't like driving the interstate. Right before we entered Nebraska we heard another POOF. We knew what that meant! Two things. Number one, we had blown another tire (actually it was the spare which had rotted out from not being used), and number two-good thing we replaced that tire! We were back on the road in no time at all! I was getting to the point that I could change tires faster than the pit crew at the INDY 500!

Dad Passes Away

My father suffered a severe heart attack in January of 1995. He survived but was confined to a bed and could only walk using a walker. I really haven't mentioned my parents too much up to this point. They were good, honest, hard working people. I did mention that my father was a used car salesman-he kept working until he was seventy five years old! My mother was an executive secretary to the owner of a manufacturing plant here in town. She retired when she was sixty seven years old. We had struggled financially for as long as I could remember. Both of my parents had jobs that paid a fair wage, but my father's drinking had held us back.

Dad struggled for the next eleven months. In November, the week before Thanksgiving, he suffered a major stroke. He would not recover from this. He lingered for a few days and passed away the day before Thanksgiving in 1995. He had always kept a very low profile for as long as I could remember. He loved to kid around and tease my mother, my brother, and myself (wonder where I got it from?) We would find out much later the reason he kept a low profile, why he kept to himself, and was an alcoholic for so many years.

Volleyball Becky

Becky had always been a very beautiful girl. She had somewhat of an athletic build-but with grace. When she was in sixth grade at Our Lady of Lourdes she joined the volleyball team. Just like all of the other Willits' she poured her heart and soul into her endeavors. She became very good very fast. I went to as many of her games as I could. She was definitely a volleyball star!

When she went to high school she made the Junior varsity team her freshman year. When she was a sophomore she played on the varsity team at the largest public high school in the state. Not bad!! She would continue to have a great high school career and was scouted by some of the colleges and universities. She decided not to go to college right after high school which she now deeply regrets. She could have made the program at some of the bigger universities.

All was not lost though. She ended up working for a professional golfer demonstrating and promoting his line of clubs and one of his driving aids. Becky would travel around the country attending all of the major pro golf tournaments and meeting professional golf's elite group. She would get a chance to rub elbows not only with the golfers themselves but with their wives and families. She learned a lot while working for this organization.

Chapter VII:
Our Second Handicapped Child

Challenge Number 5: Cole is Coming

Carole noticed right away that this pregnancy was different than the rest. She had been involved in a minor traffic accident early on but the doctor assured us that that had no effect on the unborn baby. Cole did not move around like the other children did. Carole had a test to see if the baby would possibly be a Downs Syndrome child. I guess they can do those now before the baby is born. The results were not good. The baby failed the test. At this point we were given the option of terminating the pregnancy (Carole was only 4 months along) or continuing on knowing full well that we were in for a rough road- rough road compared to what! The doctor forgot just who he was talking to or he never would have asked us that question! There never was a decision to be made as far as we were concerned. We would take the hand that God dealt us and make the best of it that we could. We were used to that. Kim was still doing great for a Rett's girl. She was still walking and she would try to feed herself if anyone made the mistake of leaving food within her reach. Boy! That girl could eat. She still can!

Carole went in for her eight month doctor visit and at that point had been having contractions. The doctor put her on bed rest for the remainder of her pregnancy. When she went in for her next doctor's visit he discovered that both Carole and the baby were in distress. He immediately sent her to the hospital. We were in the delivery room when things really started to go bad. They had to perform an emergency ciscerian section.

Cole was delivered not breathing. The delivery doctor had to resuscitate him to get him to breath. This was definitely not good! Cole would remain in the hospital for the next two weeks. He would come home for a couple of days and then be right back in the hospital.The doctors could not find the problem. The doctors also told us one more thing. Cole probably wouldn't survive the year. This was not at all what we wanted to hear. Cole definitely had his problems, but he is ours.

For the next four years we were fixtures at the two local hospitals that could handle difficult cases like Cole's. Still no diagnosis. What was wrong with him? They have a general diagnosis for babies when they can't figure out what is wrong with them-Failure to Thrive. Cole was in that category for the next four years. In 2000 the Rett's Syndrome researchers came up with a gene test that positively identified the disorder. One of Cole's doctors ordered the test for him-just another condition to disqualify. But, wait a minute. The test came back positive. Cole has Rett's Syndrome. That's peculiar. Rett's Syndrome attacks the X chromosome. The girls have two X chromosomes so the condition leaves them severely handicapped. However, boys only have one X chromosome. They rarely survive the pregnancy or live just a couple of weeks at best. But Cole is five years old!

Remember those doctors who said Cole wouldn't make it past his first year? After Cole's first birthday party they conceded that he has an extraordinary will to live. But they also said he probably wouldn't make it to five years. We reminded them of this at his fifth birthday party. They will no longer give prognosis on his longevity. The doctors continue to be amazed at his very presence! At this time he is the oldest living Rett's boy. There have been numerous studies done on him. We have had numerous medical challenges since Cole was born. From these we have learned to take life one day at a time. Our life would adjust to meet his needs. We would have something new to us that we had never had before, even with Kim. We had to have nurses in the house to take care of Cole overnight. We would have them around the clock until Carole and I learned how to care for Cole. This was a far cry from my EMT training fifteen years ago! Carole on the other hand actually was working with newborns in the hospital, just not as critical as Cole. For the next year we would be very busy learning how to handle High Tech life support systems, monitoring systems, and everything else that goes with them and him.

We put Cole in the parlor of our Victorian Mansion. It was just inside the grand entry hall on the main floor. It was a large room and everything (and everyone) fit. The nurses also would not have as far to travel unless they needed to wash out medical supplies (the non-disposable ones) or make their dinner.

I came home early one day to buy a suburban. This was our vehicle of choice after the vans-the stretch vans were just too big! I didn't get to buy my suburban that day. About ten minutes after I came in Cole stopped breathing. We bagged and gave CPR to him and got him breathing again and took his vitals. We also took his temperature. We were shocked to see that his body temperature was over one-hundred five degrees. We called the rescue squad right away. I remember while we were in the emergency room that one of the nurses was giving me a gentle back massage to keep me calmed down. That was not good! At this point Cole's temp was over one-hundred eight degrees. We found out later that it went even higher than that. Everyone in that room except for Carole and I thought he was gone for sure. We held on to the hope that he would somehow pull through. He survived the night and the next day the doctor diagnosed him with HSE. What is HSE? It's the abbreviation for

Hemorrhagic shock and encephalopathy. One of the doctors tried to explain the condition to me. When I asked about the prognosis he just handed me one of the prospectus that he got from another doctor. In the pamphlet it kept referring to the post-mortem. That's an autopsy! It seems that almost all of the healthy kids that get this don't survive. What was keeping Cole going?

Cole did keep on going. He did survive. He did lose a lot of his body functions from this disorder. He lost a lot of his mobility in his arms and legs. He also sleeps a lot more. At least he made it !Cole would get this disorder one more time and survive it the second time as well. The second time would claim most of his functionality.

Cole Willits

Carole Loses her Job!

Shortly after Cole was born Carole lost her job. Cole was in the hospital where Carole worked on the same floor where she worked. Cole was in the Intensive Care Unit.

One day her supervisor came in and told Carole that she was no longer working for the hospital. Cole was not doing very well. At that point we didn't know if he was going to make it or not. Carole's supervisor didn't even close the door behind her while talking to Carole. All of the people working at that time (Carole's co-workers) heard the news as well as Carole. Carole started crying. One of her co-workers tried to comfort her but it really didn't help. Carole called me at work that morning. She was still crying. I thought we had lost Cole. When she told me the news I couldn't believe it! She worked in a Catholic hospital which claimed to value life and family values above all other things! Yet, they fired her and didn't even close the door when they did it!

Carole had carried the health insurance through the hospital. At the time I had my own auto repair shop and was doing quite well. We suspected that the dismissal was motivated by the fact that Cole was going to be in and out of the hospital and would require a lot of expensive medical care. He would definitely be a burden on the insurance program that the hospital provided for their employees.

We Sued the Hospital-And Won!!

We felt that the hospital had violated several state and federal laws in Carole's dismissal as well as totally lacking moral character and values. It is a catholic hospital and right on the door to the intensive care unit where Cole was they had a "Hospital Mission Statement" that stated the values that the hospital held for all of it's patients and employees-many of which were violated when Carole was fired! I tried to contact the hospital administrator and left many messages, but got no return calls.

We contacted a lawyer and he felt that we had a pretty good case. We proceeded to put together the lawsuit paying special attention to the details that we felt were pertinent to not only the legal, but the moral issues involved. As it turned out it wouldn't matter.

The hospital settled out of court. Evidently didn't want any bad publicity! We received a token settlement that would not make up her lost wages, but it helped. When Cole left the hospital that time we made sure he or no one else in our family would ever set foot in that hospital again unless it was a dire emergency-one would come up much later!

This was a small victory for us. We didn't get to go to court and humiliate the hospital like we had wanted to. It would have felt a little better to have them see what it was like to have to squirm around a bit in a courtroom. When Carole called me after she was let go while in Cole's intensive care room she was devastated. But this would have to be good enough. The settlement was fair, but not excessive by any means.

I Have To Close My Shop

Remember when I said that life has a funny way of sneaking up on you? Carole had carried our health insurance through the hospital. After she was fired we successfully sued the hospital. We were buying our own health insurance now as there was no company plan. One day I got a bill from one of Cole's medical providers for fifteen thousand dollars. I called the health care provider and told them that we have insurance. They said that the insurance company had refused to pay the claim. I contacted the insurance company and they told me that we had reached our limit for this part of the policy. I thought (at least at that point) that there was a million dollar limit on each individual. I had never had to put this to the test until now! Guess who was right on this one?!

I would have to close the repair business down and look for a job-again-one that offered health insurance. I got right on at a local new car dealership as a drive train mechanic. Although I made about the same as when I was a store manger, it was a little more than half of what I made owning my own business. With Carole not working we really had to pinch pennies. It would take several years to get back on track.

Graduation Parties

By now the children were graduating from Our Lady of Lourdes (eighth grade graduation in Catholic schools is a big event) and from high school. Sometimes we would have to combine graduation parties if we had two kids graduating the same spring. The new house could easily hold over one hundred people-not even counting the porches and balconies! We would hold graduation parties at this house almost every year for twelve years.

The mechanics of putting on parties and get-togethers was automatic by now. We could buy a fifty piece tub of chicken cheaper than we could make it and it tasted great! We used the same supplier for many years. We had three large coolers that we would fill up with soda and strategically place about the downstairs and front porch of our mansion. We never cooked for these and always used paper plates and plastic spoons and forks. It was hard enough to get everything ready. We wanted to be able to spend as much time with our friends and family as possible. Cooking and doing dishes would prohibit at least some of that.

Thanksgiving, Christmas, & Easter

These are always special times at our house. On thanksgiving I start making the pumpkin pies a day or two in advance. I make these from scratch rather than using the frozen ones. You can tell the difference with the first bite! It is well worth the effort. We usually have two or three turkeys depending on how many of the kids come. We bake one and the kids bake the second or third birds as necessary. Chad is the mashed potato maker. He usually makes fifteen to twenty pounds of fresh potatos. We always have a box of instant for a backup. One year I made a cherry and an apple pie from scratch as well as the pumpkin pies. They were good but took too much time to justify. We have dinner around three PM and usually get "caught up" for a couple of hours after that. Then the card games start. They would sometimes go until early in the morning (I am usually in bed by the time they end).

Christmas Party 12/19/2010. The line to see Santa is long!

Christmas is another family get together time. Although, now that the older kids are married they have to share time between their own family, us, and their extended family. It's a bittersweet thing. We want them to respect and spend time with their in-laws. We brought them up that way.

As of this writing we still have Easter Egg hunts at the house. We will have these for many years to come as the grandchildren are still very young-and many unborn Willits' or maiden name Willits'.

The Little Things

By the time we are parents ourselves we have been through quite a bit. Good experiences as well as some not-so-good. We always remember the great times, the family vacations, events like marriages and the such. But what about the little things? They are what really help to make us who we are. They are sometimes not as memorable because there are so many of them, but, they become etched in our minds and hearts and are a permanent part of our character and identity.

For our kids the little things were and still are, going to the grocery store with Dad-would always involve a special treat. In fact it became such a ritual that we had to limit the number of "helpers" to two (that was all of the special treats I could afford!) When Carole would go shopping she would never have to look far for companionship! The same held true for those instances as well- we would have to limit the participants to two. We would also go for long rides in the country-the kids loved these.

Special dinners were another "little thing" at our house. Anytime a special event arrived for one of the children, whether it be a birthday, getting a good report card (all A's & B's), or some other kind of event that made that day special for one of the kids, they would get to pick out which dinner they wanted to have. The favorites were hamburger & brown gravy over mashed potatoes, (see recipe section), pizza-whether it would be homemade or frozen, and steak (if we had enough!)

Most of the boys had paper routes and I would get up every Sunday morning at 4:30 AM. to help stuff and deliver these with the kids. I had to get up early during the week anyway so it just seemed natural. This would continue for over twenty years, although I did get a few breaks in there!

These little things are so important because they go hand-in-hand with the big things to let the kids know that we truly do love them and care about how they feel. We go on vacation once a year, but, we go to the grocery store every week. The kids get report cards four times a year, and we find special events on the average every week or two. This is in addition to supporting them in sporting and outside activities, school projects, and all of the other "little things" that we take for granted every day of our lives and our children's lives.

Kaylee is Born

Kaylee was born in the spring of 1998. She was a normal delivery, although she was smaller than the rest of the girls. She had big brown eyes and when I first saw her I thought she looked like a mouse! That would become her nickname. I especially still call her "Mouse" or "House Mouse".

Kaylee would be the last Willits child (from Carole and I anyway!)

She would grow to be very neat and clean and take very good care of her clothes and toys. Some of her friends think she is spoiled because she has so many toys. She just takes very good care of them and puts them away so as not to get broken or lost. She still has many of the Christmas gifts that she received five years ago and more.

She loves to play soccer and she takes Taikwondo with her dad. I actually helped coach her soccer team for a couple of years. When you spend time like that with your children it is not just quality time, but it is much more than that. You get to see her develop, help her develop, and then help her friends to do the same. It was a truly memorable time in my life.

Basketball Holley!!

Holley went out for the school basketball team in fifth grade. I was shocked!! Holley is one of the nicest, least aggressive people you will ever meet in your life. How would she survive on a basketball court? She did! Holley not only surprised me, but made me feel proud at the same time. She was not the star of the team but definitely a contributor. She would take the path of least resistance (at least as much as is possible in basketball.) She was fairly tall for her age and could out rebound some of the other girls. She was also a pretty good shooter. She didn't start every game, but, did play in every game.

Her classmates made up the rest of the team. They would go on to be friends for the rest of her time at OLL. They would be constant companions on Saturday nights going to movies and the such. Some Saturday nights I would have twelve or thirteen girls in the back of the suburban going to or from the movie of the night.

Learning to Fly

I had always wanted to learn to fly. Who wouldn't ? From the time I was a small child I yearned for the "Wild Blue Yonder." My father never spoke of his time flying in B-24s during WWII, but he always had an attraction to airplanes. We used to go down to the airport and watch the planes take off and land. I suppose it was the influence of this and just being around someone so enthusiastic about flying that instilled a desire to fly in me. Dad had always talked about buying an airplane and learning to fly. It just never happened. He was barely able to support our family let alone have an expensive hobby like flying. He already had an expensive hobby. He was an alcoholic. When he finally did give up drinking they discovered that they had a lot of extra money. At that time dad was almost sixty years old and rather than fulfill a lifelong dream, they stayed with realities. They fixed up the house and bought a Cadillac-a gold one!!

It was different for me. I was a Civil Air Patrol Cadet while in high school. They would teach us to fly for free if we wanted. They didn't have to ask me twice! We started with ground school. We finished ground school after about six months. It took a long time because not everyone could make each class and we all absorbed information at a different pace. I loved it and was wondering why it took the others so long?! When it came time to actually start flying we found out that the Cessnas we were going to use, were to be supplied by the Air National Guard and had been recalled to be used as FACs in Vietnam. FACs were Forward Air Controllers. These were the pilots that would fly into hostile territory, unarmed, to spot enemy troop movements and gun positions. A lot of these aircraft were either shot down or shot up so bad they could only be used for parts. The few planes that did come back were in such poor shape that they wouldn't be good trainers.

Carole knew of my love for airplanes and my desire to learn to fly. She didn't forbid from learning. She did however, make me promise not to learn until all of the kids were out of the house-this was when we were first married. We have two handicapped children. They will never leave the house!! So much for me learning to fly!

In the late 1990's one of my co-workers was involved in radio controlled airplanes. He was reading a book about them while we were on our morning break. When I asked him what he was reading he showed me the magazine and I immediately took an interest in the airplanes. This would be neat! I could still learn the basics of flight and if the plane crashes I will live to tell the story.

Radio controlled airplanes can be an ARF-Almost Ready to Fly (come preassembled), A kit which you assemble, or a scratch build (built from plans and pieces of bare wood like the first airplanes were one hundred years ago!) I have always liked to build from kits because it is more challenging and you know what's inside the structures. At the time you could still buy a lot of R/C airplane kits very reasonably. I started out and didn't stop for 10 years.

I loved to build these. Nothing is more satisfying than to start with a box of " sticks" and end up with a very scale looking airplane. The first kit I built was a J-3 Cub. When I opened the box and looked inside it was really a box of sticks. You build in sections or parts. Then assemble the parts into sub assemblies. The final assembly is the last step which involves putting the sub assemblies together to produce a finished or semi-finished airplane. You still have to paint or cover the airframe, but, at that point it is very recognizable as an air frame.

Learning to fly them was a different story. At least when your in the cockpit of an airplane you know what you have to react to. If you run into turbulence or are experiencing engine trouble at least you know first hand what the problem is. When you fly R/C airplanes you only know what you can see. You have to guess the rest. The good thing is if the plane crashes (and they do crash no matter how skilled you are) you walk away uninjured (except maybe for your pride.) I also scratch built an airplane. It flew great!

Chapter VIII:
Moving On...

High Profile Model

Eric was in college, Todd had taken a year off to work and save up for college. Chris really wasn't interested in college as he had a good job making good money. Eric had taken a modeling course at a local modeling agency his senior year in high school. He had done pretty well in the 2 years since he finished the course. He was now doing a lot of local and regional shoots for the big stores. As I have said before, Eric is one of the most modest people you will ever meet in your life. He came home one night and as he was walking up the stairs to his room he announced "By the way. I have been selected to do a layout in Cosmopolitan Magazine". Carole and I both jumped up and had him repeat the news. "I'm doing a segment in Cosmo".

Eric never really kidded around too much (unlike me) and we knew he was serious. Two weeks later he went to New York to do the shoot. It turned out great! Eric was Cosmopolitan's Mr. Nebraska. After the shoot he did television and radio interviews with all of the local stations. He did some more local and regional modeling and then would get a big break that most all of us just dream about. Once again the television stations and newspapers would ask to do interviews with our family. Once again we respectfully declined. They had been asking us to do these for the last ten years at that time, and would continue through this day.

Portfolio, the most prestigious (and highest paying) modeling agency in the country wanted Eric! Eric would go on to sign a two year contract with them for a sum which I cannot mention (more than I would make in my entire working career!) He would have an opportunity to travel all over the world in the next two years.

Eric at that time was finishing his sophomore year at the University of Nebraska at Omaha. He was a business major-Eric had a very good business mind. Portfolio was stationed in Florida. Eric's plan was to attend Florida State University to finish up his business degree. Life after modeling.

I don't know how he would handle the climate change-no snow and ice, or sub zero winter conditions! He actually handled it pretty well. Eric made many trips in his first six months with the modeling agency. As I remember his favorite destination was Hawaii. It had been six months now and Eric had only been home one time-at Thanksgiving. Our entire family was missing him quite a bit.

Merry Christmas! Eric came home the day before Christmas Eve. Chris and Todd knew in advance that he was coming home and helped him to sneak into the house under the guise of bringing in a Christmas present for Carole. Best present she could ever get! We asked him how long he could stay. He said forever! He wasn't going back.

Eric had been working for the modeling agency for six months. He had not been able to enroll at Florida State like he had wanted to-the modeling agency wanted to be able to have full control over the models twenty four hours a day. Eric also missed his family. When he put it all together he felt the money just was not worth it. There was just too much missing in his life. Carole and I were never so happy!

Eric had walked out on the last year and a half of a two year contract for mega bucks! The agency called many times trying to get him to come back but he wouldn't go. Good for him! He had the right values. Eric settled back into life with his family and friends. He finished his Bachelor's Degree in Business and would go on to get his masters.

That Christmas would be a very special Christmas for our family. We would appreciate once again having everyone together. Holidays were always special days for our family-still are! Even after some of the kids had moved out we would still get together for most every holiday. After the kids started getting married and having their own families it would be a bit harder. We would have to share them with their in-laws. When they started having kids of their own it would be even harder. It's a bitter sweet thing. You see your kids less, but, you take great satisfaction in knowing that they are doing great and have successful lives of their own.

Mt. Rushmore Family Vacation

In the summer of 1999 we went to the Black Hills of South Dakota. We would always camp out on these trips using tents, sleeping bags, and outdoor camp stoves and lanterns. The kids loved it! It was a ten hour drive up there. We stopped the first night and camped at the Badlands National Park. It was definitely an experience to see the badlands-all of the maze-like, rocky, terrain. We kept the kids close to camp as I found out as I read about the park that there are rattlesnakes there.

We were up early the next morning to break camp and head on to our final destination. It only took about an hour and a half to get to the Black Hills. We camped in Custer State Park which is about in the middle of the Black Hills. We had never seen a buffalo (except in the zoo) and we were very excited to see large herds of them in the park. We also saw some elk herds. I had always wondered what it would be like to be a mountain man and have to hunt for food rather than go to the store. I think you would have to be a special breed to handle all of the hardships that would go with that lifestyle.

We went to Mt Rushmore and the other tourist attractions in the area. We stayed three days and then headed home. We took the "back way" home using the highways instead of the interstate. When we got to the Nebraska National Forest we stopped and spent the night. We had never been there before either. It was great! We stayed an extra day and went hiking and fishing. Holly caught her first fish there-a three pound catfish. She was using a short little three foot beginner's rod while most of us were using more sophisticated rigs. Yes. The others were a little jealous! We had dinner for that night. There was just one thing we didn't know. There were also snapping turtles in that lake-big snapping turtles! We found out when we pulled up the catfish that Holly had caught (we kept it in the water on a stringer). We found that a turtle had eaten over half of our catfish-the best half! That was going to be our dinner! We decided not to have the remaining part of the fish for dinner-didn't like the idea of sharing it with a turtle. We just didn't know where that turtle had been!

The next day we broke camp and headed home. We got home about one o'clock in the afternoon. As with the trip to the Rockies, we were once again refreshed and ready to tackle the world!

Family Values

When you have children you want the best for them. Just what is "THE BEST?" We have always felt that giving them structure (birth to teen years) and guidance (teen years to adulthood-is that a word?) is the best plan. From that point on you are just a "VERY Interested" observer. Occasionally you may slip back into one of the previous roles, but, hopefully, it will only be temporary. You can be the best parent and still a child, teenager, or young adult, can make poor decisions some of which will lead to trouble that may follow them the rest of their lives.

Our children were no angels, (although many were mass servers-I guess that doesn't count!) We had our share of what I consider to be normal kid stuff. However, I am very proud to say that none of our kids has ever mugged a little old lady, robbed a liquor store, or sold drugs on the street corner.

And last but not least-never forget to laugh. Sometimes things come up that are beyond this scope (as we have seen) but, in general when you lose your sense of humor (at least for good!) it is pretty much over-just a waiting game at that point! A good sense of humor is mandatory when entering upon any great and important undertaking such as raising a family. It doesn't matter if it's a big family or a small family-a family is a family.

Moving On Again

Chad, just like all of the other kids got his first job at the same neighborhood restaurant when he was a freshman in high school. He would work there for two years before moving on to the other family employer, a pizza restaurant. Most all of our kids would start out at the neighborhood restaurant then move on to the nearby pizza restaurant.

Chad had saved up money for a car for over a year when we purchased a 1982 Buick with a bad engine. Chris, our oldest son and I hand-built an engine for this car. It ran great and got around 40MPG in town. Not bad for a full sized car with a V-6 engine! Unfortunately Chad would lose this car in a traffic accident-the other driver would sue claiming Chad was at fault, but, totally lost his case in court. The other driver however, didn't have insurance-wouldn't you know it! We had a lot of work and money in that car and it performed great. You can't make the modifications to newer cars that we made to that one and get the same results. Oh well!! We cut our losses and started over!

Chad graduated from high school in 1999 and would get a full time job and attend college. Chad is also a very level headed young man. He also has a great sense of humor (wonder where he got that?) Not to brag or anything! Chad, Todd, Eric, and a friend of theirs would share various apartments for the next four years. It was also during this time period that Todd went to paramedic school and got his degree.

Todd Gets a Paramedic Degree

Todd had a very good job and made a lot of money while driving a truck for a local sanitation company. He never really complained about the job, but we knew he didn't like it. He wanted to go to Paramedic School. He saved up enough money to pay for his entire series of classes. He had to take classes for a year and a half. While he took the classes he worked nights for UPS. He would go on to be a supervisor for them-still is.

After he graduated from Paramedic School Todd set his sights on the next level. He spent two years taking classes to become a respiratory technician. It was a lot harder than Paramedic School. He is now attending nursing school. When he gets his RN degree (registered nurse) he can work in the emergency rooms in the hospitals and make a comfortable living for him and his family.

Soccer Coach

When Veronica was in fourth grade she joined the soccer team at school. All of her friends were on it so it seemed pretty natural. She went to a Catholic school so the coaches were some of the parents. At that time they were short coaches so the coordinator for the program asked for volunteers. I stepped up and was very up front with him telling him I didn't know the first thing about soccer (I played football and wrestled in high school and a little in college.) I told him that I would help him in any way that I could even if that meant carrying the ball bags and nets around and helping with practice.

I actually would go on to be his assistant for the next four years learning a great deal about the sport. He was not only a great soccer coach, but played on an adult league as well. He was very well-versed and we would have both good and great teams as a result. Along the way I learned the sport along with techniques to motivate the players (sometimes easier said than done!)

We started out on a very amicable basis and are still friends to this day. When KayLee our youngest "soccer player" started I helped coach her team as well. I really enjoyed the extra time that I got to spend with the kids as well as seeing them grow and develop. Anyone who has had the opportunity to spend time coaching and/or developing younger children know exactly how rewarding it is. If you were lucky enough to include one of your children, grandchildren, nieces, or nephews in that group it was very special.

Chapter IX:
Getting Serious-The Kids this Time!!

By the year 2000 Chris had met the love of his life-Tina. They would live together and later marry-still are! One day Tina's father had a heart attack-it was fatal. Her mother had eight year old twin boys to raise along with a three year old boy. There was no life insurance. She struggled and became sick herself from working long hours trying to support her three boys on her own.

Chris and Tina stepped in and took the twins into their home. They would remain there until they graduated from high school and went on to trade school. They still occasionally move back in when a job is lost or some other situation necessitates. Eventually Tina's mother would recover and the twins would go to stay with her on some weekends and some holidays. We consider the twins to be our grandchildren. They attend all of our family get-togethers and are remembered at Christmas.

Chris & Tina at the Victorian Mansion.

Becky Gets Robbed!!

At about this time Becky was working at local fast food restaurant (not the neighborhood one). She was working one night when a man came in and announced to everyone "This is a Robbery. Give me all your money!" He didn't show a gun so Becky thought he was just kidding and called him on it. At that point he pulled out his gun and Becky realized he was serious. She gave him the money and got him out of the restaurant-good thing. She called me to come bring her home as she was not driving at the time.

After she thought about what had happened she became a little nervous. We really don't know how we will react under pressure situations until the actual time or event comes along. You have to make certain decisions in an instant, but the reality is that those decisions and actions are dictated by who you are and what you stand for and have been formulated over your entire life-at least up to this point. This will surface again later with most all of our family. Becky made the right decision to give the robber the money to get him out of the crowded restaurant. She could have ducked down under the counter and been safe but then who knows what the robber would have done. She didn't freeze and handled the situation very well. I was very proud of her-not the first time and definitely not the last time!

At about this same time Katrina had met someone special. They would move in together and he would be the father of our first grandchild-Elise. Once Elise came though, he would change a bit and not be the family type person that Katrina had first met. They would end up separating. Katrina would be a single mother for the next two years. We would see that they were well taken care of.

Secret Agent Man!

We had a group of drug dealers move in to the neighborhood and a lot of the residents (including our family) resented this-good thing! We formed a special Drive Patrol Group that would patrol our streets during the higher traffic times for these activities (evening and night time hours) -it would still go on during the day, but it was especially bad at night. I had some pretty good company in this endeavor. One of the long time residents (I won't mention any names-he knows who he is) started taking pictures of the "street people." I bought a good camera with a telescopic lens, and started helping him. My camera could take close-ups from three blocks away. Definitely a good thing sometimes! These people were hard-core drug dealers. For their delivery system they used girls (also engaged in the world's oldest profession-you get my drift!) These girls didn't look anything like Julia Roberts in "Pretty

Woman". They were hard core "street girls". All of them were hooked on drugs and you could tell it just by looking at them. From their greasy hair to their soiled and dirty clothes they were obviously not "right".

Unfortunately we were sometimes spotted by these people. They really didn't like to have their pictures taken. It meant that we could identify them. That was the whole idea. We wanted to know exactly who we were dealing with in our neighborhood. We did this for about six months and along the way we managed to identify most of the bad guys and girls.

To do this we had informants just like the police use-maybe the same ones! Sometimes we would pay them, sometimes they would just be so tired of what's going on and needing help that they would give us the information for free! When we paid them we used our own money-it was usually never more than twenty dollars. One time we had to pay forty dollars but the information was well worth it. We were also accompanied on occasion by news reporters and camera people from the local television stations. One segment aired at 10:00PM Sunday night. The videos were great as were our pictures!

We would do coordinated efforts with the police and it would help some. When we started to put our "photo library " together we found that we had over one thousand pictures between us. I had a quick shoot camera that had actually caught several entire drug deals from start to finish on film! We turned this over to the police and they were amazed. They had to do their own investigation, but said that we had contributed quite a bit.

When the dust had settled the Omaha Police had rounded up and arrested the largest drug ring in the city to date-at least at that time. Fifteen people were arrested for drug trafficking from our area alone . I talked to the county attorney and he suggested that I write letters to the judges to tell what impact these people have had on our neighborhood. I wrote letters for all fifteen suspected traffickers. As a result, seven faced charges in Federal Court.

Also as a result we were featured on CNN. They did a segment on our association and did a ride-along with us on Drive Patrol. It was great!

A question many of you have asked is "did they ever try to get even?" Only one time. They kind of tipped their hand to their intentions. One afternoon, (this was a month after the arrests), two of the street dealers came up to our house, knocked on the door, and asked for some fictitious person. While Carole was telling them that she had never heard of the person they were looking inside trying to see the layout. She closed the door and called me right away.

I came home right away and arranged to take a few days off of work. I spent the next day outside doing some yard work (YUCC!) in the front of the house (the house sat up on a hill and I could see for blocks in each direction.)

I had a big "Buford Pusser" (Walking Tall) stick out of sight at the top of the stairs.

About three o'clock in the afternoon the two men who had been there the day before along with a third man came walking down the street. They stopped at our bottom sidewalk and started up the stairs. I saw them and went to meet them at the top of the stairs. As soon as they saw me they all looked at each other, mumbled a few words, then turned around and left. They never came back . I didn't even have to get my "Buford" stick. The house on 30th Avenue was set up somewhat like a fortress. It sat up on a hill and the front porch is wrap-around carved stone and goes the entire width of the house- fifty feet. The neighborhood kids used to call it "The Castle." It was set up for better security when it was built over one hundred years ago and is still functional in that capacity today.

Chapter X:
The First Wedding!!!

By this time Eric had met Jenny his future wife. They were introduced by a mutual friend and would date for about six months before getting engaged. Eric had his BA in Business Management and worked at the largest bank here in town. He had actually started there while in high school on an internship program and got back on after he left the modeling agency. Jenny was an emergency room nurse and also had a very good head on her shoulders. She owned her own home and was financially stable as was Eric.

Eric and Jenny were married at Boystown Catholic Church in 2001.

The wedding was beautiful as was the reception. Alex, Robert, Michelle, and Veronica had their first formal social event. They all looked great as did everyone! We had met Jenny's family before the wedding. They are very accomplished and down to earth. We now have an even larger extended family.

Eric and Jenny now have two boys, Evan and Ethan. Eric went back to school to get his Masters in Business Management (MBA). He is a middle manager for an international fortune 500 company. Jenny has just finished her anesthesiologist program and has 1 year of internship left.

Eric & Jenny's wedding

Katrina Meets Someone Special

In 2001 Katrina met Terry. Terry had worked with one of the other kids. They hit it right off. They would move in together and marry. In July of 2002, Jake was born. He was a big boy-just like Terry! Elise had a playmate. The next year Skyler was born. The duo was now a threesome!

Terry and Katrina would live in a house across the street from us for the next 4 years. Terry is a manager for a national pizza restaurant-the biggest one! Katrina in a supervisor for group homes for handicapped adults. Looks like having handicapped kids has had its effect on her!

2003-The Year For Weddings!!
Our Second Wedding

Chad met Amy through a mutual friend. They started dating and never stopped!Amy would come to the family events with Chad and become a part of our family. Chad and Amy got married in June of 2003 on a special cruise ship that had many on-board weddings during the voyage (I'd never heard of these before!) We didn't get to attend that one, as we would have liked to. Upon their return home, Chad and Amy had a large reception which we all were able to attend. It was great!

They bought a house right away and settled in. They spent the first year working on the house getting it ready-ready for what?? Cameron their first son was born in July of 2006. A little less than three years later he would have a new playmate. Chase was born in June of 2009. They are both happy, healthy boys. Chad has his BA in Hospital Administration and is working on his master's degree. Amy is a stay at home mom.

Chad & Amy at their wedding reception.

Our Third Wedding

Todd had been dating someone special as well. You can always tell when your children meet someone special. Their demeanor changes as well as their attitude and goals. This has happened to all of our kids. Sometimes they would tell us that they had met someone special, and sometimes we could just tell by the changes within them. Todd and Christy dated for six months and became engaged early in 2003. Christy also came from a large family. We met her family after their engagement-they are a very great and very accomplished group.

Todd and Christy were married in September of 2003. Their wedding was at the church that her family attended and the reception was at-you guessed it-Our Lady of Lourdes! The wedding was as beautiful as was the reception. They lived in an apartment for a while then bought a house-good timing! It was less than a year later that their first daughter, Addison was born. Two years later Addy would have a playmate-Zia. Two years later the dynamic duo (see the website pictures!) would become a trio. Bella was here!

To support his family Todd is a supervisor for UPS. He is also a licensed paramedic and has an RT License (Respiratory Technician). He is currently working on his RN degree and should be done in the next year and a half.

Todd & Christy with Cole at their wedding.

Travis & Jamie

Travis had also met someone special. He and Jamie had moved in together and were expecting their first child. Samantha was born in March of 2003. She looked just like her mother. The family of three would live in an apartment for the time being. In 2005 Allison was born. Sam had a playmate! Travis worked long hours as a lead-man for a national commercial building component supplier. He would spend his waking, non-working hours with his family. He was a devoted family man-just like all of the other young men in our family.

Travis, Jamie, Samatha, and Alexis with Dad at the "New House"

Chapter XI:
Mom Passes Away

My mother's health had been deteriorating steadily over the last several years. She had fallen at home more times than I can remember in the last two years of her life. She lived in the same house for more than forty years. She would not move to an apartment or retirement center. Finally, between my brother and myself we convinced her to move to an apartment in a retirement center.

One Saturday afternoon she was admitted into the hospital with difficulty breathing. Both Bob and I were there with her. We didn't realize how serious it was until we got a call from the doctor at four AM the next morning. We both rushed back up there to be at her side. We called all of our children and they came to the hospital right away. Mom was our last living parent. She passed away later that morning just one week before her ninety-second birthday.

Going through her personal belongings was one of the hardest things that Bob and I had ever had to do. There were hundreds of family pictures-some older than my brother and I! There were several boxes of papers to be gone through. In one of the boxes we found our father's service records from World War II. We think we finally discovered why he kept a low profile and had been an alcoholic for so long.

He had been awarded eight Bronze Stars. We were amazed by this as these were, and still are very hard to come by. As we read his service record and the theatres of battle that he was in, we understood a little more. He was in all of the theatres of battle in the south pacific that had the fiercest fighting-not just one or two. He would never talk about the war to Bob or myself. Likewise we never found any of the bronze stars or any of his ribbons or other awards. My guess is that he threw them in the trash as not to have any reminder of his time in combat. Dad was part of a bomber crew. He flew in B-24's in the South Pacific for three and a half years. The mortality rate among these bomber crews was between 60-70%-not great odds of returning. However, dad made it back in one piece-at least physically. It would take a lot of R&R

for him to be ready to return to day to day life just like many of the other returning soldiers from WWII and all the other conflicts. Back then they didn't have grief counselors-they hadn't even heard of Post Traumatic Stress Syndrome. They sent my Mom and Dad to Florida for a couple of months to stay at a seaside resort. That's how they dealt with PTSD back then My mother told us that Dad could not even sign his name for several months after returning home. She had to sign for him. She also said that after they came back to Omaha he would go up in his room and not come down for two or three days.

My brother Bob said it best "we are who we are for a reason."They did what they had to do and coped with it the best they could under the circumstances. They were truly a part of the "Greatest Generation."

Becky Goes to School!

Becky has met someone special as well (we can always tell!) She is working her way through nursing school. She wants to be an RN (registered nurse.) She has gotten far enough along that she got a job in a doctor's office-great for clinicals. She is a very level headed and grounded young woman. She will be able to do anything that she wants to in life.

Holley is also in the handicapped service field (is there such a thing?)

Holley works for a large care facility with many clients who are handicapped. It takes some special people to do this. She has a good backround-just like Katrina. Holley has also met someone special. That's all I can say as of this writing.

Our Last Set of Catholic School Kids

Remember when I said that the kids grow up in smaller groups in a large family? Our last smaller group, Michelle, Alex, Robert, and Veronica were all in school at Our Lady of Lourdes by this time. Michelle was having a very difficult time with school. We found out through some testing that she was dyslexic. This can be really hard to overcome and can usually be quite a learning setback. Michelle would eventually master this and continues to work through this disability. You never get over being dyslexic. It is with you all of your life. To overcome it you have to read a lot. Michelle likes to read and actually is a gifted writer in her own right.

Alex was and still is a very smart and quick witted young man. He had little trouble with school and homework and is a very good athlete -basketball and football. After graduating from high school he had a number of scholarship offers, but, instead of going away, he chose to stay close to home.

Robert was and still is his own person. He does okay in school but has to struggle a bit more than Alex. One day we noticed that he was getting bald spots on his hair. We asked him if he had been trying to give himself hair cuts and he said "No Way!" We took Robert to the doctor and found out he has Alopecia Ariata. This is a disorder in which your hair just randomly falls out-no reason-no warning. Robert would let his hair grow longer to try to minimize any noticeable hair loss. The disorder is not hereditary but does stay with you for your entire life. It comes and goes and is impossible to predict when.

Veronica has little trouble with school –like Alex. She is very feminine and lady-like. I was very surprised when she wanted to join the school soccer team in fourth grade. She was small, but very fast. She would go on to be a starter and play all of the rest of her years at OLL. I actually helped coach that team. The coaches are all parents who volunteered to help the program along. I didn't know the first thing about soccer (I had played football and wrestled in high school-30 years earlier!). Soccer had been one of those sports that had become increasingly popular in the 1980's and 90's. The head coach asked the parents for help, but, no one stepped forward. I told him that I would help as much as I could but didn't know anything about the sport. He kind of took me under his wing and taught me the basics. By the third year I would coach in his absence. I really enjoyed this. I could spend some really positive time with my daughter and help others as well. After Veronica graduated and went on to high school I would help coach KayLee's team for a couple of years.

KayLee entered OLL in the fall of 2003. She would have some difficulty when she first started learning to read and write, but would overcome this and master all of the learning processes by the time she was in first grade. All of the other parents that know her compliment her and us on her manners and honesty. She was in the school spelling bee when she was in fifth grade competing against kids two and three years her senior-she made it to the last rounds! KayLee also enjoys soccer and her friends. She and I take Tai kwon do together. She just took third place in sparring at a regional tournament. (KayLee is in the blue pads.)

KayLee at her Tai kwondo tournament. She placed 3rd-her first year!

Basketball Stars

Alex and Robert joined the basketball teams at Our Lady of Lourdes. While they weren't really stars they did very well and progressed a great deal through the process. They would play in the driveway or anywhere else they could in most of their spare time. Robert would just shoot at the basket for hours at a time. He became a pretty good three-point shooter.

When he went to high school he joined the team. The high school he went to had been state champs three years in a row and had undoubtedly, the best basketball program in the state. Robert was only five foot six inches at that point and we were surprised that he even made the freshman team. I went to all of his games. He didn't play much at first, but, as time went on he would start some of the time. Alex was as good as Robert but didn't want to play organized basketball again. It was his choice.

Another New House

We had bought the Victorian Mansion be cause of the sheer size and room-many rooms! We needed more room for our growing family. We also were looking into the future. We figured that the kids would get married (which some of them did.) We also figured that some of them would move away (which none of them did-good!)The third floor was large enough o put up two entire families if they wanted to come back for the holidays or just to visit.

As more of the kids moved out most bought their own homes, we realized that not only did we not need such a large house, but also, since everyone is staying in the area we didn't need the extra space anymore.

We downsized (not by much!) The new house was a block from the church that we were married in over thirty years ago. The new house requires very little maintenance compared to the Victorian Mansion-Thank you very much!!

Our present home.

Another Family Tragedy

In the spring of 2009 Travis' significant other and the mother of his two girls was killed in a car accident. It was very sudden. She loved her family and her family loved her! Jamie and Travis were as devoted to each other as any married couple-maybe more than some! Travis would be a single father. We have all stepped in to help with the day to day things that are involved with the raising of a family.

Travis is doing a great job with Sam and Ali. Ali will start school this fall at...you guessed it-Our lady of Lourdes. In the mean time he is still working very long hours to support the girls. He has a house. It needs some work but he gets plenty of help with it. We all see to that.

Chapter XII:
Important Stuff!!

The Secret To Having a Great Life As a Parent

When we are parents we all pass along certain things to our children. Some are wanted and some are not wanted. Your children start observing your actions and habits (=BEHAVIOR) at a much earlier age than most people think possible. By the time they start kindergarten they have already seen and heard (and will remember) your attitude towards your family (very important), your demeanor, and your work ethic-these other two items will become more important as they grow and mature. It is very important that during these early years as well as during the teenage years that you continue to provide the above mentioned items as well as support (both financially and morally), guidance in every aspect of their lives, and joy-from watching them grow as well as just having fun as a family and as individuals-very important as well! This will also help them to develop good social skills.

I have been very lucky in my vocational career. They say if you really like your Iob or profession and love going to work that it is not really a job. I am happy to say that in my entire working career (over 40 years at this point), I have only had 2 jobs each lasting a year and a half. The rest of the time I have been engaged in my career!

Things We Have Done Right!!

We have set a good example for our children by being good providers and doing what it takes to be long term in this endeavor. We have gotten up and went to work every day unless we were very ill. We stressed the importance of a good work ethic. We have been honest. We have presented a "United Front" when major decisions have been made about family policies-curfews, places not to go, people not to see, and proper dress-this has changed dramatically!

Carole and I would talk about these decisions between ourselves to come up with what we thought were the appropriate steps and approaches to these situations whether it be the afore mentioned items or disciplinary actions. We have stressed the importance of education. We have also been consistent in almost all of our decisions with very few deviations. This is very important.

Probably one of the more important items, especially as the kids got older was to "Always keep the door of communication open." We have never disowned any of our kids, "banished" them from any of the family activities or gatherings, or refused to talk to them.Probably the most trying times when raising children is when they become teenagers. At this point we lose some of our "Absolute control" as they develop closer ties with their peers. Sometimes they step outside of the boundaries that we set for them-yes, even our kids have done this! It's during these adolescent to early adult years that they are trying to "Find themselves" and discover just who they are (we already know who they are because we provided very strong examples both morally and intrinsically.)

Another of the more important things we did was to teach the kids that they have to earn their way through life. We supplied the essentials, they earned everything else. Most all of them live in their own houses which they bought the same way Carole and I did. They saved up a down payment and kept their credit good enough to qualify for loans.

One last thing. Be very careful to take time to enjoy life. There are going to be times when this will be difficult-that is when it is most important to "Smell the Roses!" Sometimes we get so caught up just trying to stay alive-survive, that we forget we have to live. We have to do the things that make it worthwhile for us. The same thing goes for our children. We need to let them live too. They will undoubtedly experiment and push the envelope a little. Let them earn your trust so when they do get out of bounds they will not be afraid to talk to you about it.

Mistakes That We Made Along The Way

There have been plenty of these! A lot of us have heard the old saying "You grow up with your children." There has never been a more true statement said by anyone! Hindsight is 20/20! That about covers the little things.

My early career as a store manager and director left little time for family vacations. I regret this above all. We took camping trips and went fishing, but, it was almost entirely one or two days trips! Not until I "Decided what I wanted to do when I grew up" and left the grocery business, did we really take what I feel are real family vacations. Up until that point I had to work almost every single weekend.

Nothing feels better or more refreshing than to just relax (anywhere but home or work!) for four or five days. It helps us to be better parents just as much as it helps the kids to realize that there is more to life than work and school. Life has a balance. There are things that we like to do that are rewarding to us. It can be a hobby, participating in sports, or extracurricular activities at school These things make the rest of our time spent at work and or school all worth while. This is nature's rule not mine! The older kids didn't get to partake in the longer vacations as much as the younger kids. This was my fault!

At times some of the kids would fall into the "wrong crowd." Usually we would see this in time to correct but a couple of times we had to take stringent measures-ban them from certain individuals or groups of kids. It never really got out of hand. None of our children really got to the point of no return in this respect.

As I mentioned before I did lose my focus for a couple of weeks one time. After I was "shaken into my senses" by my wife and kids I tried not to lose it again-at least not for weeks at a time.

How We Managed and Remained Financially Solvent

I have mentioned throughout this book how we did things. Here it is all in one section. First of all let's get one thing straight! When you make certain decisions to do things in your life and make certain plans, you automatically make other silent decisions or implications not to do other things-kind of like nature's balance in life!

If you want to have a large family (or maybe not so large) you are inherently obligated to put them first and foremost. You will see to their needs and well being first-before your own (emotionally as well as financially.) Be aware however, that before you can be anything in life whether it be a doctor, a lawyer, a grocery store manager, or even a mechanic, you have to be a person first. Just as you set the example for your children (children learn what they live-not what they are told!) by being a good provider and having a good work ethic, you are also forming THEIR character by being a happy good-hearted person (not always easy.)

We started out ahead in life. I had a good job and made a lot of money when we got married and continued to do so for the next ten years. We managed to stay ahead by staying away from the "Money Killers!" As far as we were concerned the "Money Killers" were new houses (looked great and were in great neighborhoods,) but we found our older houses to be quite satisfactory-when we did buy a newer house we ended up going back to an older home in an older neighborhood!

"Money Killer" #2-new cars or trucks. We only fell victim to this once. We had just sold our first fixer-upper house and had a lot of extra money. We bought a new car and truck the same year. We paid cash for one and financed about half of the other. We were greatly disappointed in both and sold both within a couple of years (at a substantial loss!).

When we bought major appliances we did usually buy new ones. We also bought the extended warranty with them. Having a large family you come to depend quite a bit on your washer, dryer, stove, and refrigerator. We would usually use these until they were totally worn out-scrap metal! When it came to washers and dryers we started out buying the "good" quality ones from the stores along with the warranties. As our family got bigger the lifespan of these seemed to get shorter and shorter-imagine that! One of the repairmen told us to start buying Maytag washers and dryers. They sold the same models as they put into Laundromats to residential customers. We started buying Maytag washers and dryers and have never regretted the move. They are more expensive to start with but, in the long run they outlast all of the others many times over.

The clothes that the kids would wear were purchased at the discount stores, (we loved the ½ price store type stores!), the Goodwill, or the kids wore hand-me-downs. Carole's family really helped us out with hand-me-downs. They were always nice and clean, but were never name brand (Guess, Tommy, etc.) When the children were old enough to want these they were old enough to get a job (or a paper route anyway.) One other thing, we didn't buy cell phones for the kids. This was another "extra" that they would have to buy themselves.

When the children started driving they already had bank accounts and enough money saved up to buy their first car, license plates, and insurance. From that point on they would pay for their own insurance, buy their own gas, and if the cars needed any repairs they would buy the parts. I would fix the cars for them. This not only takes some of the financial burden off of the parents but also teaches the children financial responsibility that will follow them the rest of their lives.

I did almost all of the house repairs on all of the houses. I put in furnaces, air conditioners, plumbing, and did quite a bit of rewiring. I would frame, finish, and hang doors. Along the way I had some of the older kids help me and in doing so they learned how to do a lot of repair themselves as well.

When it was time to remodel the kitchen in the Victorian mansion I priced cabinets, sinks, dishwashers, and flooring. To buy the "real" new cabinets (solid wood-not laminated particle board) it was going to be almost ten thousand dollars. One good thing about cable television is the large variety of programming available. I found several Do-It-Yourself channels that had wood working and furniture making shows on a regular basis. The internet is also a great source of information for do-it-yourself projects.

I found that I could custom-make the cabinets myself out of real wood and finish them for about four thousand dollars. That included the price of all the large woodworking tools as well. I already had a good table saw so I need a jointer, a planer (a wider one to finish wide boards), a router and router table, a scroll saw, a forty inch wood lathe, a dovetail fixture, and a mortiser (not really necessary). I bought all Sears Craftsman and Porter Cable power tools. I had to buy most of them new as their were no good used ones available. People just use these until they are worn out! I did find a good used scroll saw, but that was it! All-in-all it took me one week to make the kitchen cabinets. That included finishing as well. It only took me two days to install everything including the sinks and dishwasher. The electrical was a snap. You want to plan ahead and try to anticipate any issues that may arise.

Since the internet has come along it has not only revolutionized communication but also learning. If you have to repair anything in your house or on your car you can usually find the information on the internet. I can not over emphasize this! If you are a very handy person and want to do any kind of repairs on your own you can usually find the "How To's" on the internet. If you are not so handy but want to learn, the internet is also a great place to start. You want to start out with the beginner stuff and work your way up to the more important and more technical repairs and installations.

When it came to cooking I did all of that too. We didn't eat out very often, maybe once a month if that! That alone can save you thousands of dollars if you have a medium size family. I always wanted to get one of those big stainless steel Restaurant Stoves with a double oven. They were and still are way out of our reach financially. The good old gas stoves work just as well. Sometimes it just takes two of them to get the job done. A lot of the time we had two stoves. It has just been in the last three years that we have scaled back to one stove.

In the back I have a recipe section with some of our family favorites. They are pretty good, fairly easy to make, filling, economical, and will feed a lot of people. Aside from that I always watch the sales, and stay with the larger supermarkets. We still go through a gallon of milk a day-but it used to be two or three!!

Family vacations were very memorable not only to the kids but also to us parents as well. We would sometimes spend several months planning the trip and where to go. We always camped out. We would have the van or suburban fully loaded when we left. We didn't take cruises or fly anywhere-Carole hated airplanes! That's okay. We couldn't afford it anyway.

Our families were also very supportive. We usually had a fair savings account, but, from time to time it would shrink almost to the point of ANOREXIA! There were times when I couldn't miss a day of work because we were so close we wouldn't be able to pay a bill or eat. This most often happened around the time school starts-wonder why!!

When you make decisions to do certain things like have families (whether large or small) you automatically have made the decision not to be able to do other things such as take cruises, buy large vacation homes, extravagant ANYTHINGs, at least until later after the kids are grown up and on their own.

One last thing. Never give up. You never know how close you are to that corner that needs to be turned or that point where everything starts to flow downhill instead of uphill (in a non liquid sense!). We have been stretched so thin that we were squeaking just to get that promotion or big break the very next day or next week. We, just like many other families have been down but never out! Just remember this. The difference between a great person or family verses an average family is not how high they rise, but how quickly they rebound from disappointments and failures.

Taking Care of The Handicapped Children

I have talked about this in different places throughout the book. The first thing is that you have to make the decision whether to keep your handicapped child at home. When it is all said and done you'll only wish that it was as easy as the "Experts" said when they told you how "Hard: it was going to be. I can't make that decision for anyone except myself. Here is our approach all in one easy to read section. First of all we are a catholic family and feel very strongly about life and the responsibility to respect and sustain the gift of life that God gives us and all of our children. When we first noticed that Kim was not progressing normally we knew there was going to be some extra care and patience involved to keep her at home or just to have her around in general. Anyone who has or has been around a handicapped child either as a caregiver or a close relative knows exactly what I mean.

Parents and siblings of a handicapped child form a special bond with that child. All of our children helped us to take care of Kim. That is how it has to be if you have a handicapped child along with other children in the house. There just isn't enough time otherwise. That being said, Kim is a Daddy's Girl. Her and I have a special bond. I will feed her and take care of her in general more than the rest of our family.

When I had my brain tumor I was gone for a week. After the second day

Kim became very upset and started crying. She cried for two days. Carole called me in the hospital one morning and was at her wits end. She told me that Kim had been crying and nothing that she could do would make her stop. I told Carole to put the phone up to Kim's ear. I told Kim that I loved her and would be back home soon to once again be with her and take care of her. Carole said she immediately stopped crying. She started smiling and from then on until I came home she was alright. You have to remember that Kim's brain is still intact. The deficiency is neurological and is between her brain and her motor processes. She still knows what is going on around her.

Kim is still a joy to have around. We watch movies together and I still feed her, at least as much as I can. She laughs out loud quite a bit. I still find it odd that she can still laugh but she cannot talk. Although lately she has been forming words again. The Rett's people say that that can come and go as the kids age.

Pretty much the same is true for Cole. Cole had a very traumatic delivery. He was not supposed to survie at all let alone live to be one year old. After his first birthday the doctors said he wouldn't make it to five years old. Now they won't give any prognosis on his life expectancy. They know better!

Cole is a little different from Kim. Cole has profound medical problems. Just keeping him alive each day can be a challenge. He is on a ventilator, he has a feeding tube and pump, he is on oxygen, and he has several monitors that keep track of his vital signs. We wouldn't want the kids to get too involved with Cole's High Tech Life Support system as it is very involved. Not even all of the nurses are at ease with them. Carole is his primary care giver. She worked in the newborn nursery at a local hospital and had plenty of experience, although not this involved. It however was a good starting point for her to learn the extra processes and steps that are involved in Cole's care. I was an EMT on the Fire Department years ago and still remember the basics but since have brushed up and refreshed on what I need to know.

Just as Kim is a Daddy's girl, Cole is a Mama's boy. Not in the literal sense, but she provides most of his care and he appreciates her efforts and her mere presence. Cole has been in and out of the hospital more times than I can count on my calculator! For about twelve years we had a handicapped van that we used for these trips. We would buy a used van (an older one) and a private foundation would provide the wheelchair lift for us. We went through about four of these in those twelve years. Now there is a handicapped van service that will take us to and from doctors appointments very reasonably.

Kim and Cole are still in our care at home where they will remain for the duration.

Chapter XIII:
Therapy!!

I actually got started writing this as a type of therapy. In 2006 I was at work one day when I had a seizure. It wasn't your typical roll around on the floor with convulsions seizure. I just lost physical control of my body. I still remember everything that happened that day. I just couldn't respond or move for about 5 minutes. When I emerged and was able to move all that I remembered was that I was very tired. The rescue squad had already been called so I went in for a checkup.

They found a large growth in my head. I told the doctor that I was just getting a "Big Head!" He didn't think it was very funny-not doctor's humor I guess. He said it would have to come out and I would have to remain in the hospital until Monday when they would operate. I respectfully told him that I had a soccer game that I had to coach in an hour, and promised to be come back right after the game. He wasn't having any of it. I ended up missing the game-our team still won!

During the weekend I was very humbled by the number of visitors that I had. When we went out to eat it was usually at Wendys and I would always have a "Chocolate Frosty". All of the kids came up and guess what they brought me? I had ten Frostys waiting in the hospital freezer. It's times like that when you really know where you stand. I was very honored and humbled to receive so much attention.

Everyone was telling me how brave I was to go ahead and have the surgery. The plain truth was that as near as I could tell I really didn't have a choice. If the surgery was successful I would probably lead a normal life. If it wasn't, then I would have nothing to worry about! It was that simple-a no-brainer (pun intended!) for me. If I didn't have the surgery my condition would deteriorate to the point that it just wouldn't be worth living-at least not for me.

I remember just before the surgery the nurses and doctors came into the preparation room. I was already under the influence of quite a bit of "pain killers" –just added to my humorous nature. The nurse wrote in magic marker on the side of my head that they were going to cut the word "YES". On the other side they wrote the word "no". When they would ask me a yes or no question I would just turn the appropriate side of my head to them. I finally got them to laugh! It was right after that that they took me down to surgery. I remember waking up later that night but I couldn't speak and it was all very weird. The next morning I woke up and had a headache. Later that morning the first neurosurgeon came in. He told me that the tumor in my head was very large and resembled a crescent roll just laying across my head (different color though). He said it did not seem to be cancerous but they would send it off to be tested anyway. The only thing I knew was that I was hungry. They don't let you eat for twenty four hour before you have surgery. They said I could eat pretty much a regular breakfast so I dug in! By the time I was finished I was a member of the clean plate club!

I was in intensive care for 4 days. I went home on the fifth day. One thing that I remember was that I had to really think and search for my words just to put together a simple sentence. I asked the doctor about this and he said it would get better. He was right, it did-I let him keep his medical degree too! I also had some distant memory loss. I still remembered everything that happened when I was younger, and the stuff from the last couple of months. What I had trouble remembering were things that happened 2-10 years earlier. Some of it came back, some didn't. I had to be off of work for five weeks. I couldn't drive for three weeks. I remember when I was at home my head swelled up. I looked just like a pumpkin! I even thought I looked scary! It stayed that way for a week.

To help with my word selection and memory I started writing our family story. I started out with a six page narrative, and when I finished that I started on this, our family story in more detail. The one thing I can say is that everything in this book are things we really did and things that really happened to us. As for my therapy, well I still run across people or events that I can't remember, but they are fewer and farther between. The tumor turned out to be benign (B-9) just like in bingo!

I had done all of the cooking at our house since day one! For the first three weeks I couldn't be on my feet so the people from our parish took turns bringing dinner. It was great! It was the soccer team and a few of the other parents that did this for us. I was very humbled.

The company that I worked for was equally as supportive. They also brought dinners and lunches. The president of the company visited me in the hospital as well as many of the supervisors and employees. You never know how many friends you have until the chips are down. I found out and have been giving back to both communities as well since.

I made a full recovery. Except for the memory thing I'm as good as new-although I am used! I still carry Kim to bed at night and carry her out the next day for Carole. She's really not that heavy for a twenty four year old girl or woman-little woman! I took tai kwondo classes with Kaylee this year and even fought in a tournament. My reflexes came back to better than they were before. I guess the tumor had been affecting my brain for a while. The doctor said that it had probably been growing inside my head for years.

How Did You Come Up With The Title For The Book?

I didn't actually come up with the title for this book. Cole had a bad spell and ended up in the hospital for a couple of weeks. I had just gotten back to work from my brain tumor and had to take off work for two more weeks. One of Cole's nurses stopped by the house to get something that they needed at the hospital for Cole. We were talking about him being in the hospital again. It had been a couple of years since he had been in this time (almost a record!) She said that Cole just had to give us "One More Challenge" to conquer. The little light went off in my head! I had been wondering what I would call my book or story as it was at that stage (I had a narrative six pages long.) It fit right in and I tailored the story around the challenges that we have met and conquered over the years.

The Kids' Kids-Our Grandkids!

So far as of this writing we have 15 grandchildren. They are all just adorable! We see them on the average about every week or two. As a family we don't get together as much as we used to. It used to be every holiday that everyone would be at the house or even sometimes during the week. However, now since the kids have their own families they have to share their time between the in laws and us as well as attending to the needs of their own family.

It is a trade off. It's a bitter sweet scenario. You just can't put into words the satisfaction that comes from seeing their families-the families that they have started along with their husbands and wives grow and mature. We have truly started something that will grow and last for generations to come.

Tribute Page

Any time that you embark on a "Great and Important Undertaking" you need the help and support of others. The greater the scope of the project or undertaking, more assistance and co-operation is required. We have been very fortunate to have the support not only of our families, but from the communities that we have been involved in as well. We have also given assistance to them as well when needed and when we were able.

I have mentioned this at times throughout the book but just wanted to have a special section here to once again give thanks. To name everyone with out leaving anyone out would probably take an entire chapter by itself!

Tracy & Carole Willits.

Please visit our family website.

http;//www.thewillitsfamilyweb.com

Family Recipes

Feed 15-20 People For $20-Pretty Tasty Too

Goulash

Ingredients;

3lbs ground beef
1 green bell pepper
2-1lb bags of wide noodles-you can use elbow noodles or whatever
2-19 oz cans of tomato soup-any brand will do
Salt-I use garlic salt, and pepper-adds great flavor

To Prepare;

Cut up the bell pepper into small pieces. Brown with the ground beef. At the same, time in a large pan (I use a corn pot) bring water to a boil. Then add the noodles or macaroni. When the pasta is soft turn off the burner under the pasta and let it just sit in the pan for a couple of minutes-makes it more tender. Drain the pasta, add the browned ground beef with the pepper in it, and then add the two cans of tomato soup to the mix. I don't even warm up the soup from the can as the pasta and ground beef will do that when added. Season to taste. We still have this from time to time. It will feed 15-20 people.

Family Style Tuna Salad

Ingredients;

1-2lb bag of shell macaroni
1-32oz jar of miracle whip
10-6oz cans of tuna
1-16oz bag of salad mix-you can use a head of lettuce if you want

To Prepare;

In a large pot-I use the corn pot for all of these, bring water to a boil. Add the shell macaroni and cook till tender. Turn off the burner and let the macaroni sit for a couple of minutes to get more tender. Drain the macaroni and open the 10 cans of tuna. Drain each can of tuna and add to the macaroni. Add the salad mix or lettuce along with the miracle whip to the mixture. Stir well. This should be chilled for 4-5 hours-it's best when cold. This will feed 20+ people.

Tostados

Ingredients;

5-6lbs ground beef
3-29oz cans of tomato sauce
3-10 oz cans of enchilada sauce
16 oz shredded cheddar cheese
½ head shredded lettuce
3 fresh tomatoes cut into smaller pieces
20 fresh corn tortillas
½ cup vegetable oil

To Prepare;

Brown the ground beef in a corn pot or other large pot
Drain the grease off-be careful to get it all
Add the 3 cans of tomato sauce and 3 cans of enchilada sauce to the pot along with the ground beef.
Simmer for an hour constantly stirring
While the filling mixture is simmering it is a good time to shred the lettuce and cut the tomatoes into small pieces.
In a frying pan, ad ½ cup of vegetable oil. Over medium heat cook the tortillas just until they are tender.

Serving Suggestions;

On a plate, first ad the tender tortilla shell. Then add the filling mix-I use one ladle full for each. Then ad the cheese, then ad the lettuce and tomato. You really don't need any taco sauce with this mixture.
This will feed 15-20 people, but watch out! Some may want seconds!!

Hamburger & Brown Gravy
Over Mashed Potatoes

Ingredients:

1-28oz box instant mashed potatoes
3 lbs ground beef
5 pkgs brown gravy mix
4 cups cold water

To Prepare;

Brown the ground beef in a 5 qt dutch oven.
Drain the grease.
After it is browned ad the 5 pkgs of brown gravy mix and water.
Over medium heat the gravy mix will thicken.
Turn the mixture off .
Prepare the mashed potatoes according to the instructions on the box in another larger pan-I use the corn pot.

Serving Suggestions;

On individual plates put a scoop of mashed potatoes.
Then using a ladle, top with the hamburger-brown gravy mixture.
Season to taste. This actually is pretty tasty.
Serves 15-20 people.

Camper's Casserole—Can Only Be Made At The Campground

Ingredients;

5lbs ground beef
2 medium yellow onions
1-5lb bag potatoes (red or white)
1-2lb bag whole carrots (not the peeled baby carrots)
2-25' rolls of aluminum foil

To Prepare;

Peel potatoes, carrots, and onions.
Slice all of the vegetables into 3/8-1/2" slices.
Pull out and tear off a 1' piece of foil.
Make a hamburger patty.
Place the patty on the foil along with sliced potatoes, carrots, and onions.
Wrap up in the foil to make a mini " dutch oven"
Take another piece of foil and wrap again making sure that the seam is on the opposite side of the package from the first.
Place on a grate over an open campfire.
Cooking time will vary depending on the size of the fire.
I have had these cook in 15-20 minutes or take as long as 45-60 minutes.
When these are done the will be like individual pot roast casseroles (only with hamburger).
Season to taste, though you may not need to season it very much.
Will feed 15-20 people depending on the size of the patties.

Vegetable Beef Soup

Ingredients;

2-3-4lb chuck roasts
1 medium onion
1-5lb bag potatoes
1-2 ½ can (29 oz) diced tomatoes
2-16oz bags of frozen mixed vegetables.

To Prepare;

Peel the potatoes and cut into fairly small squares or pieces
Chop the onion into small pieces
Add everything together in a corn pot or any large pan.
Simmer over low heat for 5-6 hours-a large crock pot will also work.

Serving Suggestions;

Before serving make sure the 2 roasts are in smaller pieces
The simmering process usually takes care of that.
Season to taste.
This will serve 15-20 people

Dad's Chili

Ingredients;
5LBS ground beef
medium yellow onion
29 oz can chili beans
15 oz can kidney beans
15 oz can stewed tomatoes
46 oz can or bottle of tomato juice
4 pkgs chili seasoning mix-I use the mild or regular

To Prepare;

Chop the onion into small pieces
Brown the hamburger along with the onion pieces
Drain the grease completely
Add the rest of the ingredients into a large pot-I use the corn pot
Mix completely and cover and simmer over medium heat stirring frequently
until the top layer starts to bubble in many places-looks like a volcano!
Simmer over low heat for 1 hour stirring frequently
Turn off heat and let set for 1-2 hours-it will take that long to cool off to the
point where you can eat it.
Top with shredded cheese and/or crackers-or??
Serves 15-20 people (unless they're really hungry!)

Escalloped Corn/Escalloped Oysters

Ingredients;

4-16oz cans cream style corn
1 box 16 oz saltine crackers-store brand will due
1 cup milk

To Prepare;

In a large casserole pan or dish just mix everything together into a paste configuration. Salt and pepper to taste
Bake uncovered at 350 degrees for 1 hour (may take a little longer depending on the depth of the baking dish.
This is a great side dish for 15-20 people.

For Escalloped oysters just substitute 4-8oz cans of oysters for the corn-don't drain the oyster juice. It will make up for the cream in the cream style corn.